My Name Is Laurie

Laurie announced her name in utero
and a fascinating life path followed

RUTHANN PIPPENGER

Pippen Press 2012

My Name is Laurie
© 2012 Ruthann Pippenger. All rights reserved.

No part of this book may be reproduced in any form or by any means, electronic, mechanical, digital, photocopying or recording, except for the inclusion in a review, without permission in writing from the publisher.

Published in the United States of America by:
Pippen Press

Printed in the United States of America

ISBN 978-0-9854468-0-2

Interior layout by Darlene Swanson of www.van-garde.com

Dedicated
to the special souls
who come with "less-than-perfect"
bodies and minds
to teach us noble qualities.

Contents

Acknowledgments vii

Introduction ix

Chapter 1   My Cosmic C-Movie 1

Chapter 2   My Name Is Laurie 7

Chapter 3   To Teach Me a Lot! 13

Chapter 4   The Invisible Zen Master 21

Chapter 5   To Teach Laurie a Lot 29

Chapter 6   The Mini-Master 35

Chapter 7   Here I Am! 47

Chapter 8   Rafaeli at Work 55

Chapter 9   The Linguist, the Foodie, and the Model 63

Chapter 10   Laurie Longs to Know Her Father 69

Chapter 11   Family Court 77

Chapter 12   Tell Them About My Father! .85

Chapter 13   Less-Than-Perfect Material 93

Chapter 14   Power Inside Me 101

Epilogue 109

Appendix: Tools for Empowered Development 113

Glossary of Names and Terms 121

Bibliography 127

ACKNOWLEDGMENTS

If it takes a village to raise a child, it takes a larger village to raise a special needs child. Laurie and I are grateful for our extended family that forms our "village" and spans several countries. Leida Meijer, Donna and Michael Greenman, Anneke Kuiper, Dielly Bartels, Martin Hetem, Rolf and Kim Goedhart, Gerd Bjørke, Jan Ton, Ingrid Onsøien, Torunn Øhmann-Norén, Lars Kristian Holmsen, Endre Førland, Kerstin Kampen, Richard and Anne Moore-Boon, Mary Elizabeth Marlow, and Susanna McIlwaine have assisted us through physical, mental, emotional, and spiritual steps in our lives.

A warm thank you goes to Samuella Alston, who gave the impetus to start Laurie's story. Her timing was perfect. "When are you going to write Laurie's story? I want to know who her father is." Susanna McIlwaine, Susan Wong, Raquel Rosa, John (Bari) Ramsey, Donna (Hayat) Bain, and Patricia Morningstar supported me through joyful and agonizing decisions regarding the book. Kimberly Goedhart and Lois Williams helped me understand that I wanted to go beyond sharing sweet stories. I decided to reveal Laurie's life as a teacher of karmic lessons and soul connections. Dielly Bartels reminded me of many tales of Laurie's magic. Susan offered hours of warm support and editing. Raquel Rosa offered poignant observations of Laurie; raised questions that evoked additional vignettes; and edited several chapters. Without the rallying cry of support from Laurie's team, this book would not be complete. Carolyn Page's Daytime Writers Class helped me understand what an average reader might think about spiritual references and "hooga-booga."

Linda Hansen encouraged me to tell the whole truth for women everywhere. Through her knowledge of Mehre Baba's material, I found confidence to share Laurie's longing for her father. Susanna provided a sounding board to work through a dream that helped me decide to reveal the identity of Laurie's father. Still in doubt, I consulted the Venerable Dagpo Rinpoche, a Tibetan lama, who told me to tell Laurie's entire story and not just the sweet stories. His answer brought the confidence that I needed to complete the book in transparency.

Nicole Van Hoey did the final editing and layout in loving kindness. Trond Grøntoft graciously designed the book cover. There are others, too numerous to mention, who aided in the creation of this book. The village still works its magic.

Introduction

"If you look around you with intellectual and intuitive sensitivity, it becomes evident that we are here to help each other grow into graceful, elegant, loving and compassionate beings — light beings and beings of light!"

~Ajahn Sumano Bhikkhu, from
Meeting the Monkey Halfway

My daughter, Laurie Shanti Pippenger, is diagnosed with Down syndrome and has a magical ability to transform others. For two-plus decades friends and students have repeatedly encouraged me to write a memoir of our life together. When she was an infant, Paul Solomon, a spiritual advisor, called Laurie a child of man. He explained that Laurie belongs to the people and not just to me. So I offer you this opportunity to know Laurie Shanti Pippenger as your daughter, sister, cousin, or friend.

Half of this book relates the vignettes that Laurie's admirers have cherished throughout the years. There are sweet stories of Laurie's outpouring of unconditional love and the intriguing wisdom she imposes gently or radically on people's lives. Writing this memoir has given me the opportunity to grasp Laurie's life mission. Joyfully recalling the heart-warming stories was the simple part of writing this book. The more challenging part was revisiting the melodramatic set up of her birth, her illegitimacy, and her deep longing for a relationship with her reluctant father, a spiritual teacher.

I am a spiritual guide/coach who has spent many years working with multiple tools and techniques from psychology and several religions to reach happiness and fulfillment. My personal goal has been to integrate my conscious mind, subconscious mind, and super conscious mind into a single point. This is a worthy challenge and is what I believe is meant by the phrase, "Let thy eye be single." I waffle in this goal daily and am delighted for the few moments I succeed. As a result of my viewpoint of life, you will find many stories and references that are not logical, deductive, and reasonable. If you are not familiar with supernatural "hooga-booga," you may become as flabbergasted as I was when Laurie started to communicate with me even before her conception. When Laurie entered my body, my life became frequently punctuated with extrasensory stimuli. I include references to psychic phenomenon, karmic connections, and life purposes that may seem foreign to you.

I have chosen to write in a conversational style and hope that you find that comfortable. I think that my writing style flops from staid teacher to drama queen, with the awkward phrasing of someone who lectured to foreign speakers for 18-plus years. Please be patient. You will find an abundance of exclamations points in the text to express Laurie's zeal and dramatic flair. Unlike some people who have cognitive impairment, Laurie lives much of her life with energetic intensity and punch.

"My Cosmic C-Movie," Chapter 1, reveals how Laurie came to me after a series of events propelled me along a path far different than the one I had been treading. My choices were preparing me for motherhood of this dynamic soul. Writing has brought back the memories of goals I set, dreams I held, and prayers of my heart that led me to a flooded bridge that set the scene for her conception. With no judgment regarding good or bad, in retrospect, I know that Laurie's soul had been steering my life toward her conception. She was conceived the day after I closed my private practice in individual, group, and family therapy in New York City. She was conceived the day I moved out of New York City! Laurie's timing is impeccable and still startles me after living with her for three-plus decades.

In Chapter 2, "My Name Is Laurie," Laurie spent her nine gestational months communicating with me and others in overwhelming and extraordinary ways. These stories of inter-utero communication continue into Chapter 3, "To Teach Me a Lot!" By the time she was born, it was obvious that Laurie was a strong-willed, wise, compassionate, rhythmic, and impish person who would be fascinating and challenging to parent. Just after her birth, it was announced to me that she had many signs of a Down syndrome diagnosis and that a chromosome test had already been sent to a special laboratory for confirmation. I had been teaching in my opening lecture as a spiritual guide that special children come to teach their parents. As I held Laurie for the first time, I was aware that this powerful soul was only appearing in the guise of a Down syndrome girl. I understood that she was wearing this diagnosis as a costume in this lifetime. With tears of bliss, I told her that I was ready for our adventures together.

In "The Invisible Zen Master," Chapter 4, I share my sense of being dumbfounded by the effects she had on the community around us. She was a delight to carry around, because she brought joy and compassion wherever she went. There were many incidents when her toddler words and actions revealed a knowledge and wisdom base that could not be founded in this lifetime. Her awe and spiritual devotion at The Chicago Art Institute rocked my world. Earlier psychics told me that she was masterful. I had taken those messages with a grain of salt. Within two minutes in a museum room, I was awe struck by her vocal intonation and her movements. I witnessed that this toddling three year old had a divinely guided ritualistic history that predated my influence in this lifetime.

Laurie was not only here on earth to teach me a lot; soon after her birth, I realized that I had much to learn about teaching her if I was to be a responsible parent. In Chapter 5, "To Teach Laurie a Lot," I share opportunities presented to me by friends, religious leaders, Marcus Bach, and case workers on how I could make her life more fulfilling and richer with infant stimulation and beyond. Because we were living in a spiritual community, this learning became more mystical and fantastical than I could imagine.

Laurie was dubbed "The Mini-Master," Chapter 6, by a group of students at Carmel in the Valley Mystery School, a retreat center where I taught as a psychospiritual guide. Because I often traveled internationally to teach, Laurie had many opportunities to offer caretakers (usually fellow students) more lessons than they cared to learn. During this time frame, I experienced a "fountain of forgiveness" with the recitation of a Sufi forgiveness mantra. I experienced a washing away of slights and an acceptance of karmic circumstances. Peace generally reigned over our situation for several years.

You will find stories and tales of Laurie's charm, audacity, and understanding in Chapter 7, "Here I Am." "Rafaeli" was the Sufi name Pir Vilayat Inayat Khan gave Laurie when she was three months old. Rafael is one of the four archangels and is considered the angel of healing. From the beginning, I received confirmations that Laurie had powerful healing energies. An incident with a narrow, unprotected set of stairs in a restaurant in

Introduction

The Hague in the Netherlands set my conscious, subconscious, and superconscious minds reeling simultaneously. A comment by Laurie triggered flashbacks of many seemingly unrelated coincidences and incidents. For minutes, the flashbacks swirled at multiple layers of consciousness. My inner knowing hurled numerous flaying puzzle pieces until a solid picture of her being was formed. I understood who this masterful soul was expressing.

In Chapter 8, "Rafaeli at Work," you will find accounts of Laurie's holy "work" as she grew into her tween and teen years. Laurie inspired people through dances and songs. With compassionate touches, hugs, smiles, and kisses, Laurie uplifted and brightened the lives of thousands of people who traveled through life with her as friends, neighbors, or newly found friends—people who you and I would call strangers. Laurie is "The Linguist, the Foodie, and the Model," in Chapter 9. My career choices forced her to learn two extra languages, Dutch and Norwegian. This was challenging because of her hearing loss. Preparing food caringly and presenting food beautifully has always been an act of loving service for Laurie. The joy of meeting both Julia Child and Lidia Bastianich, her favorite chefs, at book signings, as well as her two experiences modeling in Norway, have been great highlights in her life.

Laurie's screaming desire to know her father is discussed in Chapter 10. Chapter 11, "Family Court." brought the grim reality of unproven paternity back into our lives. I promised Laurie that I would do my best to bring her into a relationship with her father, Saul Yale Barodofsky. This was happening as I was proclaiming to myself that I desired equality with men in all aspects of my life. Soon after the promise to Laurie, we moved to Norway, a country noted for practicing gender equality. Laurie and I relished living where most men and women live naturally in noble respect and equality. We enjoyed having understanding, considerate, respectful men in all areas of our lives from the green grocer, to teachers and our dearest friends. Suddenly, I was thrust into facing the uncomfortable fact that the father of my child in the United States claimed to not know me and refused to talk with me. So much for achieving total respect and equality in my life! I felt deflated. Ironically, the theme of my life's work and the name of my four-level spiritual school for adults was Peace Through Understanding!

On the old school advice of Paul Solomon, I was obediently keeping Laurie's father's identity a secret to protect his teaching career as a spiritual guide. My relevancy and teaching career as a female spiritual guide did not seem to factor into this thought process. However, my career never seemed to be hurt by my status as an unwed mother. However, the secret of Laurie's heritage seemed a bit scandalous. For many years, Laurie only knew that her father's name was Saul and that he was a healer. One day at a Sufi Camp in Switzerland, Laurie demanded: "Tell Them About My Father!" Chapter 12, explores the acceptance and support I received from our local community when I revealed Laurie's origins.

Paul Solomon explained that he thought Laurie chose this lifetime in a Down syndrome body to prove to people that much could be done with "less-than-perfect material." Daily, Laurie grapples with wary glances in public, deals with the label of her diagnosis, and manages to accomplish a great deal as an accomplished weaver. Chapter 13 describes her struggles and successes: Laurie admires others who also accomplish much with "Less-Than-Perfect Material." She adores hearing of real or fictional underdogs. "Power Inside Me," Chapter 14, covers Laurie's adult years. I included Laurie's skill in speed grieving. Hopefully, her simple, loving respect for a departing soul is helpful to you. Her joy of feeling normal, yet seldom receiving that perception from others; her caring for her colleagues; her talents, current achievements, use of insight; plus her hopes and dreams are found in this chapter.

My Name Is Laurie

I chose to write the Epilogue in free verse in reverie over a beautiful holy day–filled season with Laurie. Her phrases are evident. The extensive Glossary of Terms is included to help clarify the various esoteric references in the book. The Appendix, entitled "Tools for Empowered Development," presents techniques I used to aid Laurie's development and mine. I believe that this information is too technical and too disruptive to fit into the general text.

As I finished writing, Laurie was 33 years old. Finishing the editing proved to be a challenge; she is now 36 years old. Laurie has smiled shyly at the thought of her life story as a book for others to read. She would love for her life story to become a movie. I am conscious these days that we have all been informed through song or otherwise, that life is but a dream. Dreams are but illusions. Illusions are fictional. Fiction is literature. Literature's purpose is to inform and entertain. So, I present to you the fictional illusions of my experiences raising Laurie Shanti Pippenger in a memoir form.

Please know that my discussion of Laurie's special qualities is not meant in any way to detract from the beauty, compassion, light qualities, fun, wisdom, and preciousness of any other child. Every child is a gift. Every child is a teacher. Surely, many parents share the following thought with me:

> I adore this child
> Head leaning on my shoulder
> Life's magical gift

Ruthann Pippenger
June 27, 2012

1 My Cosmic C-Movie

"'Where have I come from, where did you pick me up?' the baby asked its mother. She answered, half crying, half laughing, and clasping the baby to her breast —'You were hidden in my heart as its desire, my darling.'"

~Rabindranath Tagore

It is obvious that Laurie and I had a date with destiny. I now know she had been preparing me for her appearance as my child many months and probably decades before the pregnancy. As I became more conscious as a spiritual guide, I understood how my thoughts, emotions, and actions through the proceeding years had been propelling me toward the desire in my own heart, motherhood. I have laughingly called Laurie's conception story my "Cosmic C-Movie."

Hopefully, as my story unfolds, you will understand why I've chosen this title. The "C" certainly can represent the comedic cosmic aspect of this chronicle. Most people are familiar with Hollywood's "B" movies—cheap, tasteless films dashed off with more shortcomings than highlights. Laurie's conception definitely did not fit my ideal, and it shocked and uprooted my entire existence. Although blessed by prayer and meditation in the hours earlier, there was more tawdriness in the encounter and unpleasantness in subsequent encounters with her father than I ever would have anticipated or desired. By my standards today, I consider my 1970s behavior immoral.

I know it was I who created the "movie" of my life, by producing it, directing it, and acting in it the way I wanted. With Laurie in my life's movie, the quality has improved amazingly, and I have often found my role a supporting one. The creation process that brought us together is an experience that continues to unfold.

Most of my lifetime, I have had a recurring thought. It is a secret longing, to be able to love everyone with a compassionate heart. For a long time, something always kept me from actualizing this longing, perhaps my timidity, my judgmental self, the coldness that would grip my heart. One or two ministers came close as compassionate loving role models for me; however, saints did not abound in my circles of living. I believed that I would not learn to love unless I experienced motherhood. At 26, I was divorced from a childless marriage; after that, a long-term love relationship never developed for me. Two of my male friends offered to father a child with me. I refused their offers, because the connections did not seem deep enough. Plus, I did not want to have a child with built in parenting challenges.

After a seven-year career as a public school English teacher, I chose my second career as a family therapist. My career goals were accomplished within three short years. I was self-employed as a group and family therapist, and I was working as a consultant to a social work agency and had lectured at several colleges. A seasoned social worker and director of her agency had called me the best family therapist on the East Coast. My ego felt boosted, yet I felt flat. Soon after that event, I wrote in my journal that my goals were accomplished. I also scribbled, "Is that All There Is?"

My Name Is Laurie

I was headed for a dark night of the soul. For several weeks I regularly found myself singing, "Is That All There Is?" Peggy Lee's rendition of the Leiber & Stoller song contains an amazing statement of this advanced but dark level of consciousness.

After discussing my boredom and mild depression with a psychologist colleague, he propitiously suggested I take a course entitled "Astrology, Numerology and the Group Process" offered at G.R.O.W. (Group Related Ongoing Workshops). We both taught at this private adult training center on the Upper West Side of Manhattan. I signed up and was relieved the teacher gave only one class assignment, "Get a psychic reading." She suggested seeing Barbara Lesnovitch. "Take a friend to take notes for you. Barbara talks fast!" I had never been to a psychic, did not know anyone who had ever been to one (that I knew of) and was resistant to go. However, I asked a friend, and off we went.

Observing Barbara, I was amused and skeptical. I could not keep myself from thinking of Carnac the Magnificent, the famous Johnny Carson bit. I have often thought Johnny's writers stole Barbara's routine. Although she did not dress in exotic turban and robes, to me she seemed strangely out of time. It was the 1970s, and Barbara dressed in nylon blouses and trim little pencil skirts straight out of the 1950s. Large rose-patterned wallpaper also reminiscent of the 1950s covered the walls.

To set the scene further, as clients entered, she gave each a small paper on which they wrote three questions. In the order of clients' arrivals, she put the papers in a metal organizer. After saying opening prayers, she answered questions starting from the front of the organizer. She held the client's paper up, spoke freely (in what I would now respectfully call a process of soul to soul connection) for five minutes or so. Then she opened the folded paper and channeled answers to the questions.

Like everyone else there that first night, I asked three very mundane questions. Yet Barbara's reading for me was extremely different from the gentle readings she did for others. In the five-minute advance reading before opening my sheet with questions, she jutted her head forward and looked at me sternly. In a firm, loud voice, she spat out, "You are an angel of God! And **don't** you forget it!" Clearly admonished, I was stunned, embarrassed and confused. I gulped and wondered what she could possibly mean. My middle-class New York lifestyle included work as a family and group therapist with some rock-and-roll-hippie-promiscuous-drugless-adventures on the side. So upon hearing this message, immediately I smiled inside and heard my sarcastic sing-song voice childishly saying, "I think I forgot!"

As my friend and I bounced down the stairs of the 9th Street Lower West Side walk-up, I teased her and said, "You better be careful how you treat me. You know you're walking with an angel of God." And then I laughingly shared my "I think I forgot" thoughts and told her I was really puzzled by the message. She told me she too could not imagine what Barbara meant. We stopped in a café, where we discussed and exchanged the notes we had taken for each other. That night I prayed sincerely that I might understand the message and fulfill my destiny, if Barbara was correct.

Years later, I understood an angel is really a "messenger of God." As one of my friends reminded me recently, we are all messengers of God. However, Barbara obviously understood that I needed a strong nudge in the responsibility department.

My Cosmic C-Movie

My friend and I went back to Barbara a month later with a new batch of equally mundane questions. In my open reading, Barbara kept writing the number 4 boldly over and over on the back of my paper. She paused and consciously noticed what she was doing. Then she said 1974 would be an important year for me. And it was. It propelled me into new interests and activities, all of which readied me to greet Laurie in my life and begin my saga as a spiritual guide. At the Arica School, I took the 42-day Arica Training, a course in "scientific mysticism." I learned to see and feel auric fields. I experienced deep meditations into different realities, chanted long hours, and changed my diet to even purer foods. My friends already considered me a health food junky. I found comfort and excitement in reading introductory spiritual texts and went to numerous lectures by spiritual teachers. Indeed, 1974 was an important year for me.

In meditation years later, I realized that one specific prayer of my heart started a domino effect, leading me to the jackpot of giving birth to Laurie. Arica students received a special invitation from Guru Muktananda. I postponed a leafing trip to Vermont by one day to attend this impromptu darshan invitation in the first week of October 1974. I was so moved by the holiness of the guru and the chanting session by his followers that I prayed to have abundant spiritual opportunities. Years later, I understood that prayer was answered rather quickly and differently than I ever could have imagined. By mid-October my private counseling practice began falling apart. In December, it had dwindled by two thirds. Because my private practice slowed down so dramatically, I had abundant time to pursue spiritual studies.

By December 1974, my life had been in flux for months. I could no longer afford my comfortable rental in Brooklyn Heights. I made plans to move into a beautiful mansion in White Plains with friends from the Arica School. The deal was cancelled because the landlord refused to rent to a "commune." I needed to live meagerly. Luckily, I could share an efficiency apartment with a friend named Shelley in Greenwich Village. My belongings were stored in a friend's barn. I lived out of the trunk of my car. Thankfully, Shelley spent many nights at her fiancé's place and provided me with much-needed privacy.

One January evening in 1975, Shelley and I ventured to a Zikr evening at the Arica Center. These gatherings included meditation, dance, chanting, and celebration of the Oneness. As I entered the room, an angular man stood at the door and then literally jumped into the room and started dancing spectacularly. I was instantly attracted to this wild and free man. Shelley and I enjoyed dancing freestyle with him that evening. The next day I began a three-week affair with Kedric. (Please do remember that this was the 1970s in New York where, as Margaret Mead stated, people come together through "sex, drugs and rock and roll." The drugs were missing in this case.)

Kedric was an actor, a dancer, and a street performer (most often a clown or an angel). I admired his deep spirituality. Daily, we meditated and danced together and talked deeply about life purposes. At one point, Kedric asked me what I would do if I became pregnant. I stated that I would have the child. If the father did not choose to be involved, I would parent the child alone. Just as I finished saying that, I felt the imprint of a very small, intensely warm hand on my left thigh. I shared my experience with Kedric and he said, "Well, I hope your choice of birth control works with us!" We both agreed that warm imprint of a baby's hand was a mysterious and intriguing experience.

Before Kedric left for home, literally a tree house in California, he encouraged my spiritual seeking. He suggested I attend a coming workshop on meditation with Pir Vilayat Inayat Khan, leader of the Sufi Order of the

West, and that I go to Sufi dancing at the Cathedral of St. John the Divine. I found it surprising that these suggestions were coming to me for the third time. Two Arica teachers under separate conditions had both given me the same advice. It was time to act.

Kedric was house-sitting for friends who "loaned" him a seat at Hilda Charlton's meditation group in Greenwich Village. Only 500 of Hilda's spiritual disciples could fit into the all-purpose room of the Catholic elementary school to chant, meditate, and hear her and her invited guests speak. The loaned space was good for four more weeks, and Kedric "sub-loaned" the seat to me. Through evenings in February, Hilda and her vibrant and multitalented students opened my mind, heart, and soul with stories of the power of meditation and pure action and, in some cases, poor karmic decisions ending in tragedy. I was reading books by Paramahansa Yogananda and Sri Chinmoy and anything I could find about the guru Swami Muktananda.

I did Sufi dancing and found it enchanting, if a bit weird. The energy of the meditation with Pir Vilayat was so beautifully still and deep, I decided to go to a camp at Woodstock in late June through mid-July. During the workshop in March when Pir Vilayat sat in front of me to give darshan, he startled, actually jumping in his skin. (Darshan happens when a spiritual teacher exchanges energy with the student while holding eye contact.) I noticed that he had not jolted when he sat in front of others. I suddenly remembered that Swami Muktananda had also jerked months earlier when he only made eye contact with me. I felt embarrassed and worried. All I could think was, "I must be really terrible to make two gurus jump." I prayed, "Oh, Dear God, purify me." Now, I wonder if they both had seen Laurie's glowing presence hovering around my auric field waiting for her opportunity to jump into life in my body. Today I even question, "Did she ask them for help in preparing me?"

I continued to read and meditate. In April, I was lonely one Sunday and started to feel sorry for myself. After realizing that I myself would advise a client in this position to call a friend whom they wanted to get to know better, I called a friend from Arica and asked if she was available. She said, "No, I'm not." She continued, "I know a group from Virginia Beach giving a healing seminar today at the Little Synagogue in Greenwich Village. You will like the workshop and the group. They are warm and friendly."

I trusted her judgment and ventured over to the synagogue. Paul Solomon was speaking. I was astonished by his brilliance. He said everything I knew about healing and more. This group was successfully using old and new tools and techniques to heal themselves and others. At my former hospital day job as Group and Family Therapy Director, my "advanced" views on healing attitudes learned from Virginia Satir were looked at askance.

This group announced that Paul would be teaching a class in Inner Light Consciousness (ILC) on the Upper West Side in two weeks. Wanting to learn more, I signed up. The course presented interfaith supernatural teachings with a Christian-Jewish base. I was thrilled with new techniques that worked instantly for me. I felt at home and comforted.

During that workshop, I dreamt that I found a baby girl dressed in white under some foliage in a friendly suburban alley. I was convinced that baby symbolized the new, purified me. Students were advised to take the ILC workshop several times to learn the tools thoroughly. During my second workshop I had a dream-vision of an enormous column of white light encompassing Paul Solomon, Alan Levy, who was the only other ILC teacher at the time, and me as we stood in a triangle. I awoke, knowing that I was being directed to become an ILC guide. The teachers' training was scheduled to begin in Virginia Beach on the day after Sufi Camp ended. I would be there.

Events continued to move rapidly. A new friend in the second ILC class was moving to Virginia Beach. He asked if I would take him and a U-Haul trailer to the beach in early June. I agreed. He paid the expenses, put me up, and introduced me to the members of his old New York City Edgar Cayce Study Group. He was the last of the group to move to the beach. They were warm and welcoming. Again, I felt at home. So, the decision to become an ILC guide and to live at the beach was concretized. I would move into an existing social structure. Besides that, I recognized the alley behind Allen's house as the place where, in my dream, I had found the baby symbolic of the new spiritual me! My plans were changing rapidly. I would close out my private practice, because everything seemed to be falling into place for new experiences.

The Conception

I went off excitedly to Sufi Camp near Woodstock, New York. The wooded hills were serene. Most of the camp participants were dressed as exotic hippie-types. There were joyful, loving faces everywhere I looked. I found it a bit disconcerting that most of the women wore graceful skirts with combat boots and smoked unfiltered Camels. Eight young men were constructing the large frame of a geodesic dome to be used as a meditation-group hall. Standing nearby, I heard the dreadful crack of beams shattering and then crashing to the ground. As I jolted toward the sound, I saw men flailing in the air and plummeting to the ground. Three men were injured badly enough that they were taken to the hospital. The entire camp was in shock.

Earlier that morning, I attended a healing workshop and was attracted to the charismatic leader Saul Barodofsky. Murshid Samuel Lewis had appointed him as head of the Healing Order with the Sufi title of Hakim. He looked and dressed like my friend Kedric, spoke like a Shakespearian actor, and presented a clear and powerful workshop. Later that afternoon, he led a healing circle for the hospitalized men and then left to attend to them at the hospital. I wondered if he was single and if he would be attracted to me. I wondered, "Had my friendship with Kedric prepared me for a possibly deeper friendship with this look-alike?"

A few weeks later, I heard in the teachings of Paul Solomon about soul groupings or soul families. When I first heard this, it sounded very strange to me, with my straight Christian background. Later, I felt that these two men were part of the same soul family and that, somehow, I had unfinished business with both of them. Kedric and I handled our friendship openly and respectfully. The story of Saul continues.

That afternoon, I attended another workshop in which the handling of emotions was discussed. I found it disappointing. It did not go deeply enough for me, a trained family therapist and primal therapist. So I spoke to the teacher, Saphira Linden. She made an appointment to discuss my questions at nine o'clock that evening in her tent in the teachers' compound. It began to rain after dinner. In fact, it poured. I had just purchased great camping rain gear and a powerful flashlight. I proceeded down the mountain to find her tent.

When I arrived in the teachers' enclave, Saphira's tent-kiosk was packed with people. She explained that it was the first planning meeting for the "Cosmic Mass" production that was to be held in New York in October. She apologized and said that we would have to reschedule our appointment, because their meeting would not be finished for hours.

As I was finding my way across a slippery bridge where the water was clapping and laughing at the top of the walkway, I heard a theatrical voice bellow out above me, "A light. A light! I asked God for a light and there you are!" I cast the flashlight beam upward, and there was Hakim Saul Barodofsky, the healing teacher. He had left for the hospital in the daylight and seemed not to have taken a flashlight. He asked me to guide him down the small cliff. I did that excitedly. It seemed propitious that I had this special opportunity to meet him. He asked what I was doing in the teachers' enclave so late in the evening and in such adverse weather. I explained. He invited me into his kiosk for temporary refuge from the storm.

As we waited for the rain to subside, we meditated by candle light. He read my palm. As he looked at my right palm he said, "You are of the Sun and I am of the Moon." I still do not know what he meant by that. To this day, I would assume just the opposite. He went on to say, "A woman like you should never be alone." **And little did I know that a few hours later I would be able to thank him, because I would never again be alone!**

The storm did not let up. He suggested I sleep on his pallet beside him, explaining he was married and had two children and that there would be no sex. I was disappointed to hear that he was married. I agreed that there would be no sex and immediately gave up any thought of a relationship with him. In the middle of the night he woke up, I thought, and began to sexually caress me. Remember, this was New York and the 1970s. By my standards as a spiritual guide today, my morals at that time would have to be considered questionable. We had sex and went back to sleep.

At about five o'clock, the storm stopped. Saul woke up and suggested that I go back to my tent early so that other teachers did not see me leaving his kiosk. It was dawn, and the birds began singing as I walked up the mountain to my tent. I felt joyful and thought, *I feel like I am accompanied by the birds of the forest and a band of angels.* I did not suspect that I had just conceived.

That afternoon I sat waiting to speak to Saul while he was giving darshan to students. I wanted to have closure and to say that I was sorry we had not kept our commitment about not having sex. His assistant shooed me away, saying that it was inappropriate to observe darshan. I left the camp to do final sessions with my remaining clients in Putnam and Westchester Counties. When I returned to camp two days later, Saul acted like he had never seen me before. I did not attempt further contact. I found it odd, I found him disrespectful, and I let it go.

In the past year, I have heard about sexsomnia. It is a condition in which people have sex in their sleep without waking up and have no memory of the experience. Finally, that has made some sense to me as a possibility of why I was not remembered sexually. However, I have never found an explanation as to why Saul did not remember my rescuing him from the cliff, his rescuing me from the flooding bridge and storm, our meditation, and his palm reading for me. Is his memory so deficient? Did Laurie just choose Saul as an out-of-laboratory sperm donor? Did we have a date with destiny to create her body? And her timing was intriguing. Surely, it was not accidental that I conceived Laurie the night I moved out of New York City to begin my path as a spiritual guide.

2 My Name Is Laurie

"It is said that the present is pregnant with the future."

~Voltaire

I traveled from Woodstock, New York, down to Virginia Beach quickly to begin my training to become a spiritual guide. That training was offered by The Fellowship of the Inner Light, a local church. ILC was a ten-session course in spiritual development. I found the ILC guide training exciting. I was delighted with my new teacher, Paul Solomon, this new community of spiritual seekers, and the new skills I was learning. Paul was offering teachers' training and an advanced ILC course simultaneously. Some of us did practice teaching. He taught classes in healing, astrology, stress release, meditation and other metaphysical topics.

Virginia Beach was vibrant with people enjoying the summer, each other and the beautiful beach. Our group kept a 24-hour prayer chain going for over a week. I did the 5:00 a.m. vigil. I was boarding at a home two blocks from the meditation room. When I finished my hour prayer time, I would walk to the beach to watch the dolphins swim south. Originally a Midwesterner, I excitedly discovered that early on July mornings they swim in a line several yards apart. They swim off-shore approximately one hundred yards out in the ocean. In the early evening, the dolphin line returns north.

At the end of the course, many of us accepted Paul's invitation to renew our commitment to the Christ by being baptized or re-baptized at dawn on the beach. Paul was in the water baptizing people one by one. As human participants we formed a circle near the breaking waters. A small group of smiling (aren't they always) dolphins came in very near to the beach, maybe twenty yards from Paul. They witnessed our actions and swam in a circle until we finished our ritual. Then they swam out to join the line swimming south. This dolphin experience felt like an unusual blessing. I interpreted it as a confirmation that this was a special path and the right path for me.

I often felt slightly nauseated during the trainings. The caterers were serving many meals of beans and rice. Beans were not part of my normal diet so I blamed this change in diet for my nausea. When the two-week training was over, I stayed on for a mini-vacation in Virginia Beach before traveling back to New York. I was exhausted, slept in each morning, and enjoyed indulging in nothing to do.

The second morning, I awoke hearing birds fluttering and chirping in bushes outside my window, the white sounds of traffic on Atlantic Avenue and, bizarrely, a voice that seemed to come from my abdomen as I lay on my side. "My name is Laurie. My name is Laurie. My name is Laurie. My name is Laurie. My name is Laurie. My name is Laurie. My name is Laurie." After some disorientation and disbelief, I startled to alertness. I was somewhat reassured that this chanting message was in my voice even though I was confused about its origin. Paul Solomon had just taught in the ILC class, "Don't trust any voice you hear that is not your own."

I struggled to make sense of this altered state of consciousness all the while hearing, "My name is Laurie." I asked myself: *What does this mean? What is this? Why is this happening? Am I really pregnant?* I had never heard of an embryo announcing a name. However, as a numerologist, I believe babies choose their names before birth and indirectly guide their parents to make the correct choice. There was nothing indirect here. This vocal litany continued under all of my thoughts. At one point I asked, "Who are you?" I instantly laughed out loud, "Well, that's a stupid question. Obviously, you're Laurie."

I tried to escape the voice through meditation. That did not work. I tried to slip back into sleep. That did not work. The mantra from my abdominal area clamored on, "My name is Laurie. My name is Laurie." In a layer of consciousness above the voice, my processing continued, *Okay, my period is two weeks late. That's very normal for me. Sometimes I'm three weeks late. I have never been pregnant. I just can't be pregnant.*

In desperation, I asserted, *If I am pregnant and I have to hear this voice for nine months, I will go totally bananas!* This emphatic burst calmed me down a bit, but still the voice continued.

Finally, I surrendered. Respectfully I said, "Okay, I hear you. Your name is Laurie." The voice stopped instantly. Relieved and confused, I fell asleep. I awoke several hours, later remembering the voice and my concession/promise to the voice and continued to deny the probability of pregnancy.

A day later, I traveled up to Pennsylvania to visit my dear friends, Richard and Madaline Jontry. Their rented home had been a Revolutionary War era inn. Brie, their three-year-old, flaming red haired, precocious daughter, and I were playing on the cool floor of the summer kitchen they used as a family room. Brie looked up at me, cocked her head and enunciated precisely, "Do you have a child with you?"

I said, "No," and then immediately began to feel guilty. After all, I might be pregnant.

So, I said to Brie, "Well, maybe I have a pretend child with me." How is that for being noncommittal?

Brie looked back up at me and asked, "Is her name Laurie?"

Shocked, I burst into uncontrollable sobbing. Richard, who was reading a newspaper in his easy chair, looked up. "Ruthann, what's happening?" I told him the incident of two days earlier in Virginia Beach. Richard assured me Brie knew no one named Laurie and there was no character on any of the few television shows she watched who was named Laurie.

When I went into breakfast feeling queasy yet again, Madaline said, "Ruthann, you must be pregnant!"

Richard and Madaline were supportive and wondered how I would handle my new situation as an expectant unwed mother. I decided to get a pregnancy test as quickly as I could. I was headed back to New York on the weekend and then scheduled to travel to the Midwest for two weeks.

In the two weeks following this incident with Brie, I fulfilled an agreement for parents of a college-age client. They asked that I help him become established in Minnesota. During that trip the only places to get a pregnancy test were at Right to Life Centers. I finally managed to get the test in Minneapolis. It confirmed I was pregnant. I decided, as I had shared with Kedric months earlier, that I would have the baby and ask the father if he wanted to be involved.

My Name is Laurie

On the way back from Minnesota, I stopped in Indiana to visit my father, Ernest Pippenger (so aptly named because he was almost always earnest) and his new bride, Shirley. My mother, Julia, died of bone cancer when I was a sophomore in college. My nuclear family consisted of a step-brother who was living in Colorado and my father who lived on a small farm on the Michigan-Indiana state line half-way between Detroit and Chicago.

This was the first time Shirley and I met in person. We had exchanged a few letters. Normally, I considered myself one of the black sheep of the Pippenger family, because my interests and life-style were so different from the farming community where I was raised. Announcing that I would become a mother out-of-wedlock, as we still said in 1975, I thought would cinch my position as an outsider. I was shaking with fright when I shared the news of my pregnancy after dinner while we were sitting at the kitchen table. Shirley understood my situation and she helped Dad get used to the idea that I would be a single mother. As she pointed out, I was 35 after all. I was grateful to Shirley and sincerely hoped that we would have a good relationship in the future. That did not happen.

I was delighted that they started to make plans to visit in Virginia Beach a few weeks after the baby's birth. I did not disturb their view of the world by talking about the details of Laurie giving me her name and the circumstances of the conception. I remember telling them that the father would not be very involved in Laurie's life. That certainly has been a prophetic statement!

After the Indiana visit, I moved my stored possessions from a friend's barn in New York to an apartment in Virginia Beach. I asked Paul to take a walk on the boardwalk with me. I was anxious to discuss my future as an ILC guide as a pregnant single woman. I was prepared for rejection. As we walked, Paul revealed he had known I was pregnant before I did! As a clairvoyant, he had seen Laurie's influence in my auric field during the ILC teachers' training. Mercifully, it made no difference to him that I was pregnant. My new life as an ILC guide would go on as planned. My first two classes to be certified as an ILC guide would be co-teaching with him in New Jersey the second week of September. He was convinced that I was carrying a male fetus. Obviously, I was sure that I was carrying a little girl named Laurie.

In late August, I knew Kedric was scheduled to be back from his summer adventures. I caught up with him by telephone. He shared he had been up and down the west coast going to Sufi Camps, yoga camps and dance camps. I told him I was pregnant with the child of a Sufi teacher, who looked like him. And he said, "It is Saul of San Francisco, isn't it!?"

I said, "Yes! How do you know?"

He said, "At every camp, people came up to me calling me Saul. We must really look alike! I've never met him. I even stopped at his bookstore, The Rainbow Bridge [at that time, one of the top three New Age/spiritual bookstores in the United States], in San Francisco, to meet him and he wasn't in."

Kedric assured me he would stay in touch with me. I am quite sure that Laurie engineered my meeting with Kedric to prepare me for being attracted to her chosen father and gene pool.

In September I traveled from my new home in Virginia Beach to New Jersey and met Paul to teach two ILC classes: a small afternoon class and a large evening class. It was an extraordinary opportunity for me. In two weeks, I taught every part of the course under supervision. Paul immediately approved me to supervise and certify other teachers. It seemed I was becoming spiritually responsible faster than I dreamed possible. As a physic, he confirmed that I had been a spiritual teacher in many different lifetimes.

Paul and I were staying in different homes. So, each evening we met to debrief at a great Greek diner and to plan our classes for the next day. One evening, Paul was uncharacteristically jerking his head. Finally, at the third jerk I asked, "Are you okay? Is anything wrong?" He appeared puzzled and peculiarly looked above or to the side of my head.

This eloquent clairvoyant looked down, stammering, "Well, s-s-ssince," then looking directly at me continued, "Well, since you asked. That's some baby you're carrying!" With the subject open for discussion, he seemed relieved and continued, "That baby keeps pulling my hair to get my attention. And he appears over your head or your shoulder as an old man. He's playing hide and seek with me. This is some wise old man you are carrying, and he has quite a sense of humor! He has very strong energy. You are going to give birth to a boy."

I was amused and puzzled about this scamp-ish behavior of this "old man" and did not really know what to think about it. I just logged the information. "No, I've told you the story of Laurie's name. I am carrying a little girl."

"No, this is a boy you are carrying."

We must have had this conversation six or more times during the remaining six and a half months of the pregnancy. He tried to convince me that, in England, boys named Lawrence were often called Laurie. He repeatedly told me that I should get prepared for a boy with a very strong personality and highly honed metaphysical skills.

Virginia Beach in the 1970s (and even today) was filled with genuine psychics and would-be psychics alike. Several times at gatherings, people came to me and told me I was carrying a powerful soul who was filled with light and that I was very blessed to be in such company. I smiled, disbelieving. Yet, I knew this kid was not quite normal in spiritual or personal energy. No one else had ever shared these kinds of stories with me about their pregnancies.

While teaching a course on Long Island in October, I was invited to go into New York City to see a rehearsal of "The Cosmic Mass" that Saphira Linden was directing. Someone arranged for me to stay at the home of Jodie Desmond, a singer and actor in the show. Jodie had participated in the July ILC training class. Jodie welcomed me and told me that she would be sleeping on the sofa in the living room. I would be sharing her king size bed with the female director of "The Cosmic Mass." She said, "You'll have a bit of privacy; I've put a line of books down the center of the bed."

"Oh, I know Saphira and am happy to share a room with her."

I thought to myself what a wonderful opportunity it would be to meet with Saphira again. Here was an opportunity to share in confidence about the pregnancy. I hoped she would know how to approach Saul and prayed she would give me advice. When she arrived after the rehearsal, I chided her and said, "I got pregnant at Sufi Camp, and you're the reason I'm pregnant."

My Name is Laurie

Perplexed, she asked me what I was talking about. I reminded her of the night of her first production meeting of "The Cosmic Mass" at camp and how she needed to cancel our scheduled session. I told her the story of meeting Saul on the bridge when I left her tent and how I spent the night with him which led to my pregnancy.

She said she knew Saul well. They studied together. She asked, "Have you told him yet that you are pregnant with his child?"

I told her, "No. I have written a letter and want to send it to him at his store, marked confidential." I shared that I did not want to jeopardize his marriage and family. Yet, I wanted to share the fact that I was carrying his child. She agreed that this was the best way to contact him. I sent the letter soon after this discussion. I was clearly left with the impression that this pregnancy would not be easy for Saul to accept.

It was not an easy or comfortable pregnancy. Like many women, my body felt like it belonged to the baby I was carrying and not to me. My body did not smell like mine nor feel like mine until Laurie was born. Like many women, I had cravings during the pregnancy. My only craving was for green olives. I would avoid aisles with olives in stores. If I could not resist my yearning, I would buy the smallest bottle available. I could not stop eating olives until a bottle was empty. Years later, I found it fascinating that Olive is a Bach flower remedy that Laurie always tests in need of. The reference for Olive is exhaustion and tiredness, which might have to do with the endocrine imbalance Laurie experiences. I also burped hundreds of times a day during the entire pregnancy, which was very annoying. It was an interesting experience to silence numerous burps while leading meditations as I spoke into a microphone. It was an additional talent I developed.

During the pregnancy, I drove alone back and forth from Virginia Beach to New Jersey, Long Island, and Yonkers several times to teach ILC classes. I played the radio to keep awake through the times I yearned to stop for pregnancy naps. I discovered that if I played rock and roll, which I still enjoyed, Laurie would kick me hard, un-rhythmically, and seemingly with disapproval. In self defense, I often found a classical music station on the radio. When the classical music reached her tiny in utero ears, she would kick or tap gently against the womb wall exactly in time with the rhythm. We were both happy. I never considered she would be a percussionist, I knew she would be a dancer. This "discussion of music" we held nonverbally was more verification that this was some determined soul coming to be with me. Inside me was an opinionated being used to having his/her own way! She was already training and preparing me, and I was learning to work in cooperation with her.

I lived with Paul's private secretary, who later became his wife, in a two bedroom apartment in Virginia Beach. One day as we discussed the coming birthing of our new roommate-to-be, Sharon said, "You know, God only gives you what you can handle, Ruthann."

Literally, I swooned; dropped back into the rocking chair my friends had given me at the baby shower and exclaimed, "Oh, my God, I can handle a lot." The truth hit me. This was no normal being or child. Suddenly I became more serious about my date with destiny. Throughout the pregnancy, I ignored my own thoughts that for years had been repeating in my head, "You have to have your children before turning 35 or you will have a Down syndrome child." Half way through the pregnancy I turned 35 years old.

Laurie's future godfather, Paul Edward Ricioppo, "Eddie," showed up at church one Sunday morning very confused. He had a dream, which he insisted we had to talk about. He dreamed my baby had been born and was dressed in a snowsuit and was an "Eskimo." He asked if Laurie's father was Asian. I assured him that her father's heritage was Russian-Jewish. We were all puzzled about Laurie appearing in the dream as an Inuit for weeks. Our confusion was ended when Laurie's diagnosis as Down syndrome was announced by the obstetrician. Eddie carried Laurie more than one time in his son's hand-me-down ice-blue snow suit looking very much like an Inuit with her typical Down syndrome slanted blue eyes looking up at him!

Because I was thirty-five years old and suffered from severe edema, I had been red-filed, deemed high-risk, by the doctor. I was ordered not to work for the last two months of the pregnancy. I had no savings, no support, and no income. This meant that I had to go on welfare, something this Indiana farm girl never wanted and never believed would happen to her! My need was obvious, and I slowly adjusted to the fact that this had to be. I was being trained to think positively and to accept help.

It was near the end of the pregnancy that an ultrasound revealed that Laurie was in a feet-first position in my womb. The doctor told me we had to schedule a C-section on March 15. After privately doing the numerology in my head, I looked askance and told him, "There is no way this child is going to be born on the Ides of March." I did not share my beliefs with him. From her communication with me and others, I knew Laurie was too determined to have a #5 destiny number. She would be a #1 or a #11 or a #22 destiny number.

He smiled, "Well, that's when you're scheduled. You need to show up in the afternoon of March 14."

I entered the hospital as directed. They took an X-ray to know where to make the incision. Within an hour, the doctor literally came running into my room with the X-ray in his hand. A plump nurse was comically trying to keep pace with him and was waddling behind him. He exclaimed, "See what your meditation has done! Your baby is positioned perfectly for natural childbirth." He sent me home for a normal delivery, warning me that I had 14 days to enter labor. I took his advice and walked on the beach daily with anticipation.

I had prepared my room to include a lovely nursery area for Laurie. Earlier, I had only put in readiness the girl clothing that had been donated to me. Friends in Virginia Beach and in the workshops I taught had been very generous donating beautiful clothing and baby furniture. At this point, I thought maybe I should be willing to welcome a baby boy just in case Paul was right. So during this extended waiting period, I put equal amounts of male and female clothing in readiness.

Thirteen days later, I entered labor. Nothing much happened during the night. On the morning of the 29th, another X-ray revealed Laurie was in a breech position. This time she was sideways, and I was told I would be having a C-section. I asked for a spinal block so that I could be alert to welcome Laurie into the world. As Laurie was pulled from the womb, the doctor assured me that my baby was a girl. I smiled, because she sounded like an agitated parrot. The nurse quickly passed Laurie in front of me so I could say, "Hello, Laurie. Welcome," and then rushed her away to clean her up. The doctor and nurses exchanged some muffled words that I could not make out.

And then I realized it was just as I imagined; this wise and willful being was born on a day adding up to #11 with a #1 destiny number. She would be a creative innovator who loved beauty and she would be a leader. I drifted away as the sedative kicked in.

3 To Teach Me a Lot!

__Children with special needs, such as Down syndrome, usually come to teach their parents great lessons.__

~ Paul Solomon

I awoke several hours later as my clean-cut, 32-year-old doctor came into the room and sat on the bed. He held my hand, bowed his head and cried. "We're quite sure Laurie is Down syndrome. I am so sorry. A blood sample for a chromosome test had been drawn and is being sent to a laboratory in Atlanta for testing. The results will be back in four to six weeks." My fantasy was that he thought it was a tough break for an unmarried, 35-year-old, educated woman starting a new career as a spiritual guide to have the burden of a special needs child. I didn't cry. I comforted him. Then a nurse brought Laurie to me.

For nine months, I had either been hearing or saying in introductory ILC classes, "Children, such as those with Down syndrome, usually come to teach their parents great lessons." So, I was not shocked. In an odd way, I had been prepared for this announcement, and I felt honored and blessed. I remembered the incident with my roommate and the rocking chair. I knew that God was not giving me anything I could not handle.

When they brought Laurie to me, she looked me directly in the eyes. I fell even more in love than I had been with this powerful, wise, communicative soul who had touched my heart and soul so often for months. I whispered to her, "I guess you've come to teach me a lot."

And I swear to you, she nodded her head. And then I thought, "Oh, man, am I in for it now if this soul manages to nod this weak little baby head!" And then I said to her, soul-to-soul, "I am ready."

The days in the hospital, the only times I cried were when I looked at other little baby girls and realized that they would have many more options in life than Laurie. I thought that she would not be able to marry and would not be as free to live a life that I thought she might want. I can still cry about that alone once or twice a year. I vowed to myself and her soul that I would protect her from pain and sorrow and from people who might unintentionally hurt her.

Actually, about two times a year at Laurie's initiative, we cling to each other and sob intensely about her missed opportunities. Because Laurie is high functioning, she clearly recognizes that the children she was raised with are now living widely differing lifestyles than she is. The first hurdle she missed was being able to drive a car. She probably could handle driving in the country, but she would never manage in Washington, DC, traffic. She longed to go to college. Those kids she was raised with now have live-in partners or are married with children, have college degrees, have careers primarily in education, and have been through several cars. Laurie always confirms that, in her next lifetime, she will be an actor, a model, a dancer, and a great doctor. God bless her in those pursuits!

My Name Is Laurie

A matter-of-fact pediatrician came into my hospital room the afternoon that Laurie was born. He told me that, because the doctors were quite sure she was Down syndrome by the shape of her neck, the shape of her hands, and the Simian line in her palm, she might not be able to nurse. Defensively, I said, "She will nurse. Believe me, she will nurse." All I could think was that, if an animal can nurse, Laurie can nurse! I could not resist showing him the Simian line in my right hand.

In Indian palmistry the Simian line, a symbol of combined head and heart function, is considered a sign of harmony and wisdom. Almost all Down syndrome people have this crease in their palms. It crosses from one side of the palm to the other about an inch and a half below the base of the fingers. In humans it is more usual to have separate lines of head and heart, as described in palmistry. I have met several spiritual teachers who also have Simian lines in their palms. In Western palmistry, a Simian line is considered a symbol of misfortune and weakness. The Western thought is that it is a sign of weakness if one's thinking and emotions are a unified force. I personally believe that only by bringing our thoughts and feelings into balance can our eyes ultimately become single with our spiritual/holy nature.

Laurie had jaundice and stayed in an incubator when we were not together. The nurses were fabulous. They guided Laurie and me to ease the nursing. They confided that they were praying for us. I was relieved and happy and smug that Laurie was actually nursing within twenty hours of birth. That's good progress for any child. I was discharged, but Laurie unfortunately needed to stay in the incubator. Friends drove me from Virginia Beach to DePaul Hospital in Norfolk, a distance of eighteen miles, to nurse Laurie twice a day. The pediatrician whom I mentioned earlier saw me rocking and nursing Laurie in the hospital nursery. He smiled as he walked by and said, "I heard Laurie is nursing easily. I thought the two of you might prove me wrong!"

During that first interview with this doctor, I was also insulted when he warned me that Laurie might not be able to discriminate. I took it in, doubted it, and certainly thought about it. Most often it came to mind the many times Laurie would lovingly latch on to and hug someone whom I did not want touching my child. However, I learned that her sense of discrimination is flawless. She knew who needed her warm feelings of compassion.

Being estranged from my family and having lost my mother while I was in college, I had no family members to help me after giving birth to Laurie by C-section. As I think about it, it is not so much that I was estranged; it was that the family was miniscule by this time. My mother out of irrational emotions made sure that we were not very close to my father's relatives, even though several of them lived nearby the family farm in Indiana. Anyway, they were struggling in life to make ends meet and were busy with their own families. All of my grandparents were deceased. My maternal great-uncles were deceased and left no children. Shirley, Dad's bride, was working, and I did not know her well enough to ask her to come. My mother's twin brother and only sibling, EC, had passed away. I was not close to his life partner. His ex-wife, my favorite aunt, Mary, had passed away. Gene and his sweet wife Doris lived in Colorado, raising their three kids. It was not until my late 30s that I understood that it had been my role as the eldest female to keep the few strands of the family close after my mother died. At 19 and as a busy college student, I did not recognize that responsibility. The family splintered. Only Dad and I maintained our contact with Sunday evening telephone calls.

My dear new friends in Virginia Beach cared for me as I recovered from the C-section. They cooked for me and strengthened me with little-known exotic herbal teas and porridges recommended by Edgar Cayce readings for healing and nursing. All of this was bizarre for me yet warmed my heart daily. I am forever grateful for their sacrifices and loving attention.

Within the first two weeks, a friend and I were talking about my situation and Laurie's uninterested father so far away. I had not received a response to my letter from Saul. We both agreed that I should dare to call Laurie's father at his store, alert him that his child had been born, and ask for his prayers for Laurie. With shivers of nervousness, I called his bookstore. I asked if he was in and if I could speak to him confidentially. This I am sure was not unusual, because he was an established spiritual guide. When he answered, I came straight to the point, explaining that I was the woman who wrote the letter in the autumn explaining that I was pregnant with his child. He snorted, "I never received a letter like that before!"

My sarcastic Scorpio self could not resist zinging back, "Well, I certainly hope not!" Thankfully he did not hang up.

I explained that Laurie was born and was diagnosed as Down syndrome. He repeated five or six times, "It's all very interesting. I will pray for you and the child." That was it, end of conversation. Obviously I was disappointed. He gave no indication that he remembered our meeting. However, I felt strangely relieved that this well-known and respected healer would be praying for Laurie and for me.

I had not been around many babies in my life. It was a new-found and exciting experience for me to watch people's reactions and responses to her. When Laurie was two weeks old, I was driven into Norfolk, a seaport, to take care of some business. The driver and I were not familiar with the neighborhood. I was suddenly tired and hungry. My friend stopped at the nearest café we found. As we walked to the café, an elderly Catholic priest with a grey pallor stopped us to look at Laurie. He seemed to pink up a little as he smiled and said, "Oooooooo, she's cute. Bless you and the child."

I sat facing the back of the café. There were some very painted ladies at two booths at the rear of the restaurant. At first I was shocked and then realized that we were close to the docks and that Norfolk is a harbor town. Prostitutes were inevitable in this neighborhood. The women noticed that I had walked in with a tiny baby. Two of these women came over and asked to see the baby. As I unwrapped Laurie, they literally cooed, "Oooooooo, she's so cute." I then realized that a baby fresh from heaven had the same effect on the priest as it did on aging prostitutes. The sound from both the priest and the prostitutes was exactly the same, a sound that reverberated and opened their hearts! I was enjoying motherhood, learning a lot, and feeling blessed.

When Laurie and I returned to the hospital for her first check up, a handsome Iranian pediatrician who must have been forty years old was in charge. He introduced me to a student he was coaching and asked if I agreed for the student to observe the examination. I agreed that the student could join us. Laurie was lying nude on the examining table. He was coolly ignoring Laurie and energetically explaining about Laurie's chromosomes to the student. The results of Laurie's diagnosis had just been confirmed by the laboratories in Atlanta. Rapidly he was sketching chromosome symbols on the paper covering the examining table. Two minutes later Laurie peed. Her urine spilled over the table onto the doctor's slacks. He looked shocked, paused, then laughed knowingly. "She's taught me a lesson by peeing on my new slacks. I shouldn't have spoken of this in front of her." He then gently touched Laurie and said, "Forgive me. Thank you for reminding me to pay attention to my patients."

I teared up and thought of what a wonderful, respectful, wise man he was to ask an infant for forgiveness. I admired him for admitting that he could and should be open to learning from an infant.

The doctor explained to me that the chromosome test revealed that Laurie has a rarer form of the syndrome called mosaicism. Not all of Laurie's cells are trisomy 21. He shared that approximately one third of her cells are normal, and that would mean that she would be higher functioning than the nondisjunction trisomy 21 in which the "error" is copied in all cells. It was also at this time that he explained that her heart and lungs were perfect and that she would have a normal life expectancy. I was relieved. We went home to begin our new life together with this diagnosis.

In those early weeks, only one twenty-something man asked me what was "wrong" with Laurie when he looked at her. Paul Solomon overheard him and came back to me and said, "There is nothing wrong with Laurie! She has chosen to express in this body. It is not wrong. It is a soul expression and a soul choice. It is right. Everything is right with Laurie." Those words have been extremely helpful and empowering to me throughout the years.

Dressing Laurie became a fascinating task for us each morning. One morning when she was three weeks old, I was dressing her for church. She was happily on her back on the bed after bathing and diapering. I was being very indecisive about choosing one of three outfits I was holding for her. She started cooing and waving her arms and legs. I smiled and cooed back. And then, I noticed she was only looking at one dress. *Ding Dong! I got it!* She was communicating her choice to me. But I could hardly believe this. So, I put one dress down, moved the two dresses around in my hands. Yes, even behind my back! Then I held those two dresses in front of her. She did not waiver. She continued to look at her original choice. "Okay, Laurie, I understand you have preferences! (It seems that I quickly forgot how strongly she expressed preferences in utero about music and rhythm.) You get to choose your clothing from now on."

Even later, when she was too short to reach her closet, I would choose two outfits, place them in front of her and she would make her choice. We almost never had arguments about clothing.

Our life in Virginia Beach was exciting in the weeks after her birth. That summer Virginia Beach seemed to be overpopulated with good vagabond musicians. I was deeply touched and amazed that two songs were written for Laurie within the first few weeks of her life. She had a following! It was obvious that I was seen as Laurie's mother, rather than that she was seen as my daughter. One song was written by a close female friend and the other by a young male troubadour congregant in the Fellowship church. I regret that I never had the songs recorded for Laurie to hear later. I was given the words of one song at one point and, in all of our moves, I lost the verses. The songs opened many people's hearts and were sung at the church and gatherings at the beach that Easter. It was obvious that Laurie was touching people's emotions and thoughts. At this point, I was often stunned by her effect on individuals and groups. I seemed to be there to transport her and to learn.

Happily, Kedric Wolfe—my eccentric and now platonic Californian friend—visited us. He had kept in touch by phone. That summer of 1976, he had been at both the Republican and Democratic conventions doing street theater. He dressed as an angel, using high-tech fabric and structure for graceful wings. He swept up debris in front of the convention centers. *Time Magazine* had covered his mission as a symbol of warning to both parties of the need to clean up the planet and society. I was proud to be his friend and appreciated that he cared enough to visit us for several days.

Kedric sang and chanted to Laurie, massaged her with his giant hands, and enjoyed her hot little healing hands. We laughed about the first time I felt her hand on my thigh a year and a half earlier. For several years, he sent loving messages and birthday cards and presents to Laurie. Kedric's understanding, wise, and gentle involvement was welcome, tender, and sweet. When Laurie was fourteen, we connected for one day at an amusement park in California. We later lost contact while traveling/living between the Netherlands and Norway. We have reconnected on Facebook. Kedric remains dear to our hearts.

Baby massage was all the rage in the mid-1970s, and I learned to massage Laurie. Paul gave me specific guidelines for keeping Laurie's neck and pelvis loose, warning me that the diagnosis could limit movement in those areas. So, every evening when I was with Laurie after her bath, she received an oil massage. Like everyone else in Virginia Beach, I was addicted (still am) to the Edgar Cayce massage oil Aura Glow. Those precious moments of massage relaxed both of us and provided a peaceful bonding. I surmised that not only the cool temperatures in our Dutch home but also her increasing body awareness motivated her to request this ritual to stop at age eight. Her love of dancing has kept her neck and pelvis very loose. (There is information on the massage in the "Appendix: Tools for Empowered Development.")

When Laurie was in the womb, I had chanted to her for hours on end. It helped relax me and helped me deal with my situation as an unwed mother. I could feel her settle down in the womb when I chanted, and I also became quieter. After her birth, I sang many lullabies to her as well as chants and religious songs. The first time I started to sing "This Little Light of Mine," I was appalled at the limiting words I had sung all my life. Who in any point of wisdom wants an iddy biddy light? Especially when those of us who have studied Christianity have been taught as recorded in John 14:12, KJV, that "...He that believeth on me, the works that I do shall he do also..."

I realized you cannot do great works with a little light. I decided to teach Laurie that she possessed a great light! So, I changed the words for my family and for gatherings. We sing, "This Great Light of Mine, I'm going to let it shine!" This is ILC in action.

Another teaching from the ILC class became ingrained in me within weeks of Laurie's birth. That teaching is the Universe loves to fill a vacuum. It is nearly impossible to leave a drawer or shelf empty. The Universe wishes to fill it. It amazed and delighted me to learn that, if I emptied Laurie's closet as soon as she outgrew one size and gave those clothes away immediately, beautiful clothing of the perfect size came in through the door in a day or two. (There is more information on manifestation in the "Appendix: Tools for Empowered Development.")

As an infant, Laurie had a little indoor swing that she adored. One day while cooking, I draped a scarf I had been wearing over a supporting bar of the swing. Suddenly I heard her laughing loudly and giggling. She watched it closely for many minutes at a time. She was catching it, fondling it, and obviously enjoying seeing it drape, move, and glide with her movements. Her adoring godmother, our apartment mate, and I laughed with her and caught her infectious joy. For weeks, we each contributed different scarves so that she would have some variety in texture and pattern. We were careful that she could only catch it with her hands and not get entangled in it.

After several weeks, Sharon said to me, "I just have to say this! I've been thinking for a week Laurie must have been a silk or rug merchant in her last lifetime." It was obvious that Laurie loved fabric and silk especially.

I was surprised two years later when I discovered that her father's new business in Charlottesville, Virginia, was the Sun Bow Trading Company. He is a rug merchant—a dealer of tribal and nomadic rugs and textiles!

When she was two years old, we lived in a small apartment above a dress designer/tailor. One day we were fortunate enough to meet the owner on the street as she was unlocking the door. I told her that Laurie always stopped to look at the beautiful dresses on display in the window. Now that I think about it, I am quite sure the owner must have recognized Laurie's hand and nose prints on the window! I told her I hesitated to bring Laurie in and asked if she approved. She welcomed us warmly and warned, "Do watch out. There may be pins on the floor."

The walls were lined with typical banquette tables that the designer used for cutting patterns. Bushel baskets under every table brimmed with multi-colored scraps of fabric. Laurie would scurry from one basket to another. Smiling, she would literally dive into the baskets feeling the textures, smelling the fabrics and rubbing them with her hands and against her face. She laid them out on the floor comparing or matching them. She was never bored. I would have to disrupt her "work-play" so that we could go upstairs for dinner. Little did we know, Laurie would later study textile arts and crafts in Oslo, Norway, and become adept in fabric arts as a teenager.

The owner was also a student of expanded consciousness and development. We enjoyed our discussions. She obviously enjoyed Laurie's enthusiasm and interest in fabric. They hugged and kissed often. I was uplifted when she asked if she could keep Laurie on her church's prayer list.

Laurie was about seven months old when her godmother and I took her on an outing to Williamsburg, Virginia. Nearly everybody stopped to say, "Hi," to Laurie, who was riding and smiling broadly in a baby carrier on my back. They would invariably say to her "You're so cute!" It finally became a joke between us. Laurie's godmother was convinced that everyone would say it within the first minute they met Laurie, and she was right. We heard the positive mantra, "You're so cute" to her or "She's so cute" to me for many years. I think that phenomenon stopped when Laurie was ten years old and possibly lost some of her innocence.

A year later, I took Laurie to Williamsburg in the summer time. At seven months she had jumped for joy in her carrier back pack many times during a tour of the Abby Aldrich Rockefeller Folk Art Museum. She waved excitedly and jumped up and down while viewing several paintings. I had purchased several prints and tacked them up for her. When we revisited the museum, she was once again enthusiastic.

As we left the museum, we walked past the swimming pool at the Williamsburg Inn. Laurie wanted to get into the water. I did not have a swimming suit. Two pre-teen girls were playing with a black stone. One would drop the stone in the water and the other one would dive and retrieve it. Laurie found the game fascinating. She waved and smiled wildly, indicating that she wanted to get in the water with the girls and share in the fun.

One of the girls held Laurie and the other one handed her the stone. Laurie handed it to the other sister and this went on two or three times. Then Laurie purposely dropped the stone in the water and the sister dove for her. She was delighted. The sisters reversed roles. People started watching the smiling endearing child with the cute and attentive girls. Laurie began to notice the other people in the pool. Beaming she handed the stone to a person next to the girls. The stranger handed it back.

Laurie's infectious smile and giggles began to attract more attention. Sweet laughter and many smiles were happening around the pool. Laurie handed the stone to the next person in the pool. Sometimes she would toss it gently for the person to dive and retrieve it. Soon Laurie was being passed from person to person, hugging and kissing some and always smiling and giggling. She was passing the stone to each subsequent person in the pool or inviting them to dive for it. Within fifteen minutes she had been carried around the entire shallow end of the pool. Almost everyone in or around the pool was watching her. From a chaise lounge, I watched Laurie enliven and harmonize the occupants of the pool. Twenty minutes earlier they were an aloof group of upper middle class tight family groupings, and now they were a unified group, sharing, smiling, laughing, and—oh, yes—saying, "She's so cute!" The sisters were glowing with pride. Laurie had worked her magic, and it was time to go home. I witnessed her bring love and joy into fifty people's lives in a few minutes. It was an honor and a pleasure to transport her to do her work.

For the first eight years, Laurie was dressed like a millionaire's child. With her smiling face, lush brown auburn hair, sparkly blue eyes, and slightly olive skin, no one could resist Laurie as she pranced and flaunted around in white or pink dresses. At four, she had forty child-chic designer dresses, all in the same size. I was overwhelmed with the gifts from two little girls from wealthy families, each with two sets of indulgent grandparents. I calculated that there was no way she could ever wear forty prissy party dresses before outgrowing them. It was far too many dresses for one little girl to own. I split the wardrobe of dresses in half. I knew Laurie's preferences of color; however, I allowed her to make the final cut of those she would keep and which twenty dresses she would give to her brown-eyed friend Tara.

One of the hardest lessons Laurie taught me was that I was not more important to her than anyone else. Laurie loved everybody equally. I only remember three exceptions in her early life when she expressed strong dislike toward someone. I imagine that her rejection was a teaching from her to them. I watched other Fellowship babies demand that only their mothers pick them up. They would not go smilingly to strangers. It often broke my little tin heart that Laurie would enjoy Paul, or Suzie Q or Mary-so-and-so and Tom, Dick, and Harry as much as she enjoyed me! It took several years before I could accept the fact that Laurie loved everyone unconditionally. Ultimately my jealousy pangs disappeared. I often regret that I am not as loving and demonstrative as Laurie is. Possibly, as I get older, I can be the wild little old lady who is terrifically demonstrative with her love. I laugh and question how ancient will I have to get, since I am 71 now.

4 A Private Zen Master

***Oh, Dear God, I don't know what she just did or said,
and may I be that wise with my parents in future lifetimes.***

We moved to Newport News in 1978. I accepted a position there as a family and group therapist at Alternatives, a drug treatment center for teenagers. Many of the clients were referred to us by a court. However, none of our clients were hard-core criminals. Several of the staff members were disciples of the deceased Indian Guru Meher Baba. It was a warm pleasure to feel at home with colleagues interested in holistic techniques of group psychotherapy and family therapy.

Thankfully, Laurie was emotionally open to changes. In the early years, she adjusted quickly to new people and places. Laurie was in an intellectual program that needed three adults to move her body in a creeping or crawling movement five times an hour for five minutes, three hours a day. This put me in need of three volunteers a day to aid Laurie's mental, physical, and social development. I called several local churches to ask if they had a group who would be willing to take Laurie on as a healing project. A local Baptist church agreed. A volunteer coordinator from the church signed up five volunteer patterning teams for the weekdays.

We found a reliable babysitter who amazingly did not mind being visited daily by three volunteers from a local church. In fact, I think she liked the company and the excitement in her home. One person would move Laurie's head and the other two adults would move her legs in the appropriate manner. This process, called patterning, is considered important for development of the brain and for helping individuals overcome intellectual disabilities. (Patterning is introduced more completely in the chapter "To Teach Laurie a Lot" and is expanded in the Appendix.)

There were times when Laurie needed to go to a nearby childcare center in the afternoons. The babysitter's daughter picked Laurie up on the nights that I led group therapy. Otherwise, I picked Laurie up. On one of those evenings that I was to pick her up, the center was closed. I was shocked. Where was Laurie? Wasn't it my day to get her? Had someone else picked her up? It was one of the busiest intersections of Newport News; the shipbuilding shifts were changing, and traffic was glancing by in all directions. Panicked and shaking with fright, I looked around the playground and the outside of the building and the intersection. I did not see her anywhere. I was terrified and frantic! I checked if she was at the babysitter's by error and she was not there. I called the director of the center. She said, "I'll meet you at the center in five minutes. I am so sorry."

In those minutes, I was praying for Laurie's safe return and making all kinds of deals with God: "You return her and I'll go back on the road. I rededicate my life to you and Inner Light Consciousness. Please, please, return Laurie to me."

When the director met me at the center, we opened the door to find a cleaning staff person holding Laurie in her arms. She had come in to clean the center and found Laurie in a back room. Laurie had managed to crawl up into an adult size rocking chair. She was rocking herself and whimpering fitfully. It was obvious that she had been crying for a very long time. Her face was puffy and red, her eyelids were spotty. I was so relieved, and my heart went out to her that she must have felt so abandoned by everyone. She melted into me and gasped huge gulps of relief. The error had happened because Laurie had fallen asleep in the back room earlier in the day while being patterned by her volunteer team. The patterning team had left her there to finish her nap. The staff forgot to check that room before they locked the doors and closed the center. The next day, and ever after, there was a sign in/sign out sheet for parents.

A week or so after that, Laurie and I were headed for church when I spilled an entire cup of 7-Eleven coffee down the front of the white skirt I was wearing. By the time I returned home, rescued the skirt from the stain, and changed my clothes, it was too late to drive the forty-five miles to church in Virginia Beach. So Laurie and I went to the park to play. It was an intensely bittersweet day for me. I knew this time of being together and being able to enjoy her everyday was coming to an end. In my heart, I knew that an international teaching career was beckoning me. She seemed more adorable to me than usual that day. I absorbed her energy, her face, and her temperament deep within my being. I took many pictures. She was a delight of walking and beginning running skills. She pretended that she could reach high enough to unlock the car. She smiled and touched my face often with her little hot healing hands. Each time, I felt her blessing me. In the pit of my stomach, I knew our relationship was changing. My heart ached. I understood that we each had spiritual work to do that would separate us.

God had heard my wheeling and dealing! Or, Laurie had set the whole thing up so I would get serious again about my spiritual responsibility, as Paul Solomon called it. Within weeks I was having dreams of returning to teach ILC and going back to the Fellowship. I had a vision/dream in which the Holy Mother blessed me for future spiritual work. I felt my cells vibrating for a week after that vision. I had dreams that I was teaching in Europe. Years later while teaching in Europe, I actually experienced déjà vu and recognized some of the rooms. I announced at the counseling center that I would be leaving my job in five months to return to teach ILC. This meant falling short on a commitment to the center to stay for five additional months after that to lead a program in family life education that I had designed. The boss was furious and told me that I could not stay another five months. I was to leave at the end of that week.

I had been living hand-to-mouth with no savings. We were lucky enough to live with a friend for the next five months before I could take the advanced teachers' training. Then I would be booked for ILC classes. I managed to sell a few Avon products and discovered that I was not a salesperson! I did not dare apply for another job at my level of competency and then drop it in five months either. It would not be fair to any agency to do that. I knew of no temp agencies that offered family and group therapy. After those five months, I sold my car to pay back my friend for room and board during those long months. It was a sweet time to be with Laurie, but it was a difficult time financially.

At this time Laurie used little language. Typically she would say, "Mama," "Bye-bye," and "More." "More" was one of her favorite words. I always teased her and said she was "More-ful." More raisins, more sliding, more swinging, more stories, more dancing, more hugging, more singing, etc. Laurie said "more" more than any other child I have heard then or since.

I had a small altar in our room. There were pictures of Jesus, Paramahansa Yogananda, Swami Sri Yukteswar, Lahiri Mahasaya, and Babaji (not the 20th century guru) of that same Indian yogic line of teaching. One evening Laurie climbed up on my lap, put her arm around my neck, looked me in the eye, and said distinctly and decisively, "Mama, Babaji is Jesus." I was blown away first by her use of language and second by the solemnity and depth of the teaching. I said, "Thank you, Laurie." Babaji reportedly appeared over and over to spiritual teachers and their students and lived for centuries. Reports were that he miraculously lifted small groups of advanced students in India on clouds from one area to another to teach them in remote mountain areas. With Laurie's four words, I realized that this revered Hindu saint could possibly be a reincarnation-expression of Jesus. Her comment opened the idea that the same emanation of God could and would minister appropriately in different cultures.

When Laurie was about twenty months old, a friend who had been observing Laurie in playtime activities pointed out to me that she thought Laurie experienced instant karma. This woman found patterns of Laurie's play with other children amazing. I was not convinced. However, I had noticed that if Laurie was a bit naughty with another child she often suffered as a result. If she looked angry or "said" something in anger or punched someone in anger, she immediately would trip and lose her balance or run into a shelf and bump her forehead. The more I observed her playtime activities, the more it did seem that she had her own private-personal-mini-Zen Master following her around. It was indeed as if an invisible Zen stick tripped her or pushed her if she was unkind to a friend. I noticed other toddlers in play groups from spiritual families, and this did not happen to them. It was as if Laurie had an agreement with her soul to remind her human self to let go of negativity and only share love. This pattern continued until she was eight years old, when we moved to the Netherlands. Possibly, by that time, she learned her lesson. Plus, the Netherlands is a softer culture with, in my opinion, less prejudice, less competition, and more respect than stateside culture. I think she learned that she did not have to step over someone to express her power and leadership. In the Netherlands, Laurie learned to lead in a way that benefited everyone.

When Laurie was three years old, we moved from the Norfolk, Virginia, area up to the mountain community Carmel in the Valley at Timberville, Virginia. This was the home of the advanced teachings of The Fellowship of the Inner Light. At the beginning in 1979, there were approximately one hundred twenty members. There was a large southern mansion where meetings took place and staff worked in offices. There was a smaller newer mansion called Hearthfire Lodge where The Synthesis Program, a four-week advanced psychospiritual study was held approximately six times a year. Community members lived in small farmhouses on the property or in the nearby town or in two old motels that we rented. By early 1981, the group dwindled to approximately 25 members because of in-fighting and financial problems. The large farm was forfeited. From 1980 to late 1983, Laurie and I lived in the nearby town of New Market on the second floor of a converted carriage house, usually with an au pair.

I was on a teaching tour in Chicago. Laurie was in the nursery school at Carmel in the Valley and was being cared for by community members. At Easter time, she was to be brought to me by the caretakers, who were taking a Midwestern vacation. The week before, I had awakened with a terrifying dream regarding Laurie being injured for life. I called her caretakers immediately. "Be very careful watching Laurie. Don't let her out of your sight, please!" They scoffed at me and assured me they always watched her carefully. Defensively, I told them I almost never dreamed of Laurie and this dream was not symbolic. It looked real. I prayed that they would really listen and asked God that, if Laurie had negative karma, it could be lifted. I prayed that any negative karma would pass, be nonthreatening, and be learned in an easier way than I had seen in the dream.

My Name Is Laurie

Their trip from Virginia was delayed. They were hours late delivering Laurie to me at our designated meeting spot—my father's farm outside of Orland, Indiana. They stopped long enough to hand her and her bag out of the car to me. They cautioned me to be careful when handling her, "She has a second degree burn on her chest."

"What happened?"

"The soup pot had just come off from the stove and Laurie was first in line. She wanted to see what was being put into her bowl and tipped it down to look inside, the hot soup dumped on her. The just-boiling soup soaked through a little nylon shirt (which they added to her wardrobe in my absence) that maintained the heat until we could rip it off." And I immediately and silently thanked God. It was a mild injury. The prayers for lightening the injury had worked!

My Chicago hosts had invited and warmly welcomed Laurie into their home. They were extremely generous and offered me the use of their new Jeep to go to the Art Institute of Chicago. Laurie loved museums. I had not been there for years and wanted to share the collection of impressionistic paintings with Laurie.

Because it was Easter vacation, the museum was packed. As I made my way to the information desk for a map of exhibits, Laurie dropped my hand. A half minute later in the line, fear flashed through my solar plexus as I realized she was gone. Thankfully, she was wearing a red velveteen coat and was easy to spot. I saw her racing around people's legs. As gracefully and considerately as possible, I raced after her. Like a cartoon character, I dodged around people shouting, "Excuse me!" over my shoulders.

When I reached her, she was standing in the middle of a nearly empty room looking upward. She was turning reverently in a circle with her arms raised in a V above her head. She was whispering in a Sufi chanting style, "God, God, God." The sound was "Gawd, Gawd, Gawd." I was amazed at her peculiar behavior. I looked up to discover what she was seeing that was inspiring this peculiar behavior. I was stunned. The room was filled with tall, slender Buddhas that towered above me. At that time there was no statue of Buddha at the Fellowship even though it was an interfaith church. I knew we had not seen one on anyone's altar. So, the only word in this lifetime she had for Buddha was God.

In those few moments, I realized this daughter of mine was a being who not only recognized this spiritual master but was devoted to and enraptured by Buddha! It was as if she was playing out a ritual or holy dance. I could only imagine that she had been a very devout Buddhist in the not-too-distant past. I felt touched by this innocent expression of worship and her delighted surprise to be in the presence of the representation of her obviously very beloved guru. When her twirling and chanting was finished, I held her up above my head several times so that she could enjoy the statues from a higher viewpoint. We stayed there absorbing the energies until she was ready to move along.

When we left the museum, I bought Laurie a bag of chips at a kiosk on the way to the parking lot. We were almost to the car when again I noticed that she was running away from me, back to the snack kiosk. In amused frustration, I ran back. As I approached the kiosk, a grinning man was handing her another bag of chips. Internally I was going, "Oh, no!"

I went all the way back to pay him. He graciously shared that when she got to the kiosk; she looked up at the clerk and said, 'More" on tip-toe. This man laughingly bought her another bag. She tried to turn in her empty bag just as she brought empty dishes back for refills at the community dining hall. Charming Ms. More-ful had struck again!

About this same time, I had taken Laurie to a very highly recommended pediatric ophthalmologist. Laurie clearly did not like her prescribed glasses. I thought this was just because glasses are cumbersome and difficult to learn to wear. She often took them off and left them in some obvious place. A community member would usually find the small pink pair of glasses and return them to us within an hour. And Laurie's little face always dropped when they were handed back to her. I became suspicious when the glasses were lost for an entire week. Finally someone found them tucked under the leaves of a very verdant plant on the veranda. A watering can had clicked against the glasses and given away Laurie's chosen hiding space. I discovered how spunky and clever my two-and-a-half year old really was. Her cleverness had purposefully and skillfully managed to get rid of the hated glasses. Obviously she hoped to be rid of them for once and all! She was teaching me to listen to her nonverbal communication—the glasses were not correct.

This time I found a local optometrist to help us. He confirmed that the glasses were terribly wrong for her eyesight. Laurie was delighted with her new glasses and only took them off carefully at naptime and bedtime. Obviously, she did enjoy seeing clearly!

While we lived in the community in the Shenandoah Valley, Laurie was also teaching me daily in small ways and continually in large ways. Certainly there was the lesson of believing in myself, trusting God would provide for us, and learning not to be negative in adversity. In the warmer months, people streamed in from around the world to take our advanced retreat, The Synthesis Program. I was on staff and/or directing the program and received a modest salary. It puffed up my ego to teach advanced ILC to students coming in from four continents. I did not look for full-time employment, because I did not want to jeopardize my study and international teaching possibilities.

Carmel in the Valley was under great economic strain in the winter, when there were no classes offered. It was cold and barren financially. In October and March, I often taught in Europe and came back with income that I could stretch for several weeks. Generally in winter, I was on welfare, heat assistance, and food stamps and barely existing. It was an effort to find money to buy paper products and soaps. Sometimes, I did not even have a quarter to buy Laurie a small bag of chips. I often thought that I should write a book about the hardship of welfare mothers. Unfortunately, I never felt the urge or found the time to follow through on that project.

In early 1980, I felt desperate enough to go to the Social Services department in Woodstock, Virginia. I told my young social worker that I had heard that Laurie's father had moved to Virginia. I requested the department ask him to take a blood test to determine paternity. I hoped that they could prove paternity to get some financial support for Laurie. She agreed emphatically that someone should go to Charlottesville and said that she would probably be sent to meet Saul.

A couple of weeks later, I visited Laurie's nearby school in Woodstock. I dropped in to talk with the social worker on my way home. She had not called me with feedback.

She sweetly and immediately apologized for not getting back to me. The social worker assured me that she had gone to interview Saul. Then she said that he told her that women students often became enamored of him and that he did not know me. She continued, "He does not recognize your name. He has no idea who you are. Therefore, he **cannot** be Laurie's father."

Now, this was before DNA testing. She had not insisted that he take the then-current blood test. She actually cooed, describing his wonderful, exotic tribal rug store. She enthusiastically told me how hospitable he had been. She raved that he served her tea out of an authentic Russian samovar. "Can you believe he actually has one? Isn't that amazing? He was so charming. He's such a gentleman." She smilingly repeated, "He was so charming."

I was stunned and questioned, "You do **not** believe me and you did **not** ask him for a blood test!?"

She simply said, "No, there is no need" and then emphatically declared, "He does not know you!"

The inference was that I was lying or crazy. I was wrong and he was right. He was an exotic successful merchant and charming. I was broke and taught at the weird spiritual community down Route 11. She assumed, as she said he had inferred to her, that I must be just an infatuated student whom he could not remember.

I am quite sure there was no infatuation the social worker could read in my demeanor. I had explained that this was a one night stand. I did not argue. She was immovable. I left thinking that this must be God's will, which does not mean I was not upset. I have often been upset with what I thought was God's will.

During the twenty-mile drive home to my apartment in New Market, my pre-ILC temperament and Brooklyneze came back. I alternately kept screaming or muttering to myself, not without humor, "I f**kin' know how charming he is! I'm the one with his kid!"

I am not proud of the fact that I probably also labeled the social worker a stupid bitch. I forgave myself for sending her negative energy. I then worked at forgiving her for being so gullible and dismissive of me. When I shared this saga with friends, we wondered how many other women had been dismissed and disrespected by that social worker, that office, and the state of Virginia.

On the ride back, I remembered Saul's palm reading that night of the conception in his teacher's kiosk: "A woman like you should never be alone."

I chuckled to myself as I often did and, speaking to Saul soul-to-soul, said "Well, thanks to you, Saul, I am not alone!"

And I thought to myself, *I am really glad for Laurie. She is a gift from God.*

Soon, I traveled more internationally and our circumstances became more fortunate. When I was about to travel, Laurie enjoyed the excitement of the trip preparations. She observed me packing and unpacking often. She wanted to help and demanded to pack independently. At the beginning, she managed to find plastic bags, soft bags, small bags, big bags, and she filled them. She became a magnificent packer. She became a habitual packer. She became a daily packer.

A Private Zen Master

Both the au pair and I were continually aggravated to find our possessions and the pots and pans disappearing. To survive the daily onslaught of packing, we devised a system. We put a small overnight bag and two cardboard boxes filled with clothing she had not grown into yet and my out of season casual clothing in the bottom of a closet. This was on Laurie's path to and from her room to the rest of the apartment. Laurie quickly understood that this was her packing area and her packing material. Everyday Laurie packed and unpacked to her heart's content. After she went to bed, the bags were emptied; the boxes were refilled and ready for the morning ritual to begin.

Laurie has often served me as a Zen Master. She has taught me much about assertion in two ways: one by allowing me to observe her in action and two by my having to hold my own with her powerful will. She demonstrates inner strength beautifully. Since the age of eight, Laurie has claimed that "power" is her favorite word. Before eight, she demonstrated this characteristic without verbalizing it. Interestingly enough, I think she does not choose the word love because she is love. Laurie does not recognize love as separate from her being.

On a one-day break from a European teaching assignment, we went to a small French circus in the south of Belgium. Laurie was nine years old. A five-foot-tall male clown selling popcorn kept insisting that I buy from him. I was being too polite. He persisted by actually pushing the box hung around his neck, holding bags of popcorn, firmly against my body. I kept backing up and shaking my head no. Huffing, Laurie rushed to me. With disgust, she pushed the box and the clown away with her left hand, forcefully put her right hand up like a traffic cop across the box and shouted in his face, "No! No!" He instantly got the message. As did I!

One of the lessons that Laurie has taught me, I hope, is deep within my subconscious and will pop up when needed. During times when I was being very parental or scolding her in conversation, she would look me in the eye and answer with such brief wisdom, self-respect, and certitude that I did not know what hit me. I would find myself experiencing a dazed state, my parental ego feeling shattered. She would be sure of herself, assertive and not aggressive. For an example, she might remind me that I was as angry at myself as I was angry at her behavior. I would be so awe-struck by her stately presence that her words would not stick in my mind. After her short lesson, I could only say, "Thank you, you are right, Laurie."

Laurie's remarks have often stunned my logical mind and ego into a state of numbness. I have also experienced this phenomenon of a seemingly empty conscious mind during deep regression sessions and meditations. After these moments of her insights, I remember that I prayed numerous times, "Oh, Dear God, I do not recall what she just did or said. May I be that wise with my parents in future lifetimes!"

Often people say to me, "You are so patient!" Patience is certainly a trait that almost all parents of special needs children develop. Laurie has given me many opportunities to learn patience, and I am sure I have taught her the same lesson.

Laurie has taught me to be more assertive by dealing with the infamous Down syndrome characteristic of stubbornness. If you believe in astrology, please note she is also an Aries with a Taurus ascendant, which enhances the desire for leadership and willful control. For years, I struggled to hold my own with this enormous power of hers. When Laurie was eight, at the advice of an acupuncturist (who several people told me was the greatest healer in the Netherlands), I wore a black pearl. She said it would make me more assertive. I immediately bought one and wore it for two years. I became stronger. It worked because black pearls actually do help you develop assertiveness or because I believed it would work. My role as the head of our two-person family finally seemed concretized.

Both Laurie and I were born in the Year of the Dragon in Chinese astrology. So, when we come to strong disagreements over power and control, blasts of fire fly furiously. This must happen three or four times a year. It is a fearful sound for anyone to witness. Laurie's stepfather quaked the first time he observed our standoff. (I was married briefly to a marvelous Norwegian colleague, Endre Førland.) Laurie and I almost never use put downs, yet we forcefully express our thoughts, feelings, values, and wishes. Usually, by the time our dragon fire and smoke clear, we are both satisfied and state to the other how we will each resolve the situation. If either of us has insulted the other, we immediately and sincerely apologize and ask for forgiveness. Peace reigns again in the Pippenger household.

Gratefully, Laurie has also taught me a great deal about ending disagreements quickly. My parents held grudges against each other for decades! They held grudges against each other's relatives for decades! Laurie teaches the opposite. She almost always settles disagreements with friends, colleagues, and family within moments. She forgives and hugs instantly. Knowing her exacting memory for most details, I am sure she does not forget. She is mindful of what happened and will be aware of how to skillfully approach a similar incident with the same person with more attention and care. I remember once being stunned and concerned with one incident Laurie had with a small playmate at age three. Laurie's aggravation lasted about twenty minutes. It was a relief to me that this was a one-time episode.

I often have said that I have had two teachers of love—my father and Laurie. My father taught me hatred, distrust, and disgust on Monday through Friday, as he returned from his factory job, bellowing prejudicial judgments worse than Archie Bunker in *All in the Family*, a 1970s situation comedy. I literally shuddered daily at his ranting when he returned from work. He worked in a team with first- and second-generation Europeans. When I met these men as a teenager, they told me what a nice kind man Dad was. Now, I suspect he took his frustrations of being bright and in a menial job out by screaming hateful epitaphs about these men to Mom and me. These fellow workers were individuals he had not been given permission to honor by his conservative culture. As a child, I understood that his ranting was what not to do. Of course, my mother reminded me often of this. I know that, by the monkey-see monkey-do phenomenon, I absorbed some of his judgments even though I made efforts to never repeat his insulting verbiage and lack of respect. I vowed to learn to love all nationalities. In fact, my mother was my third teacher of love. She often repeated the adage to love all people, although she could not seem to model that teaching.

Laurie and I live in a building with five hundred five condominium units. We live in a rich, multicultural environment. This is in a community where one middle school has an enrollment noted for the eighty-six different languages the students can speak. We both enjoy the excitement and surprises that diversity offers. Walking down the hall after being in a multi-language-culture-color elevator group, Laurie often says, "I love ALL people!" Laurie models acceptance, trust, and compassion every day of the week. I am grateful to walk through life with her.

5 To Teach Laurie a Lot

*"Don't believe what your eyes are telling you.
All they show is limitation. Look with your understanding."*

~ from Jonathan Livingston Seagull by Richard Bach

Parenting Laurie brought more learning to both of us than I could have ever imagined. Laurie's soul seemed to be teaching me indirectly to aid her.

Because of Laurie's diagnosis, people were incredibly helpful to me. Many people gave suggestions to make our life together easier. I was grateful. Almost everybody in our immediate network was interested in lifelong learning and superlearning, the use of multi-sensory techniques to learn large amounts of information quickly and easily. Being the parent of a special child in this environment brought many opportunities to learn new skills. Our church community cared deeply for this adorable, happy baby. They offered tools and techniques, some of which had science behind them, and many techniques that seemed very strange to me. For instance, one woman presented a tiny cap to Laurie. The woman made the cap that she had heard and seen in meditation. It was much like a dark blue yarmulke with a golden pentacle inside a triangle. Laurie was to wear it an hour a day and it was to enhance her energies. I must admit, she seldom wore the cap because it continuously slipped off.

In 1976, it was an opportune time to be raising a child with cognitive impairment. Large quantities of funds were released at the city, state, and federal levels to programs for people with special needs. At six months of age, Laurie was in "school" two mornings a week. This infant stimulation continued twice a week for her first two years. Obviously, I was learning about infant stimulation also. She learned to creep by wearing rubber-toed sneakers (for traction) while stretching for raisins. I believed that Laurie would thrive best with me, her Masters Degree in Education teacher/mother, working with her constantly in the early stages. It was a special time. Laurie would seem to meld into my energy field several times a day. I felt incredibly blessed and happy. It was an active time for me with Fellowship studies and with stimulating Laurie. Occasionally, I taught an ILC class and did some counseling.

A church member told me about broadcasting. With this too-simple-to-be-believed mystical tool, you are allowed to speak to and influence your child's subconscious until the age of seven. I excitedly learned that a child's subconscious is most receptive the few minutes before sleep. I was quickly convinced that broadcasting would work for Laurie. I was haggard from her awakening throughout the night. After two ten-minute sessions of broadcasting to Laurie at three-and-a-half weeks of age, she started sleeping through the night, each and every night! What a relief. We both enjoyed a full night's sleep!

My broadcasting nightly to Laurie became a sacred ritual and continued until she turned seven. At each stage of her development I would say an affirmation that encouraged and empowered her. It went something like this: "Laurie, you are a child of Light, a child of God, you are loved by God. You are now learning to crawl.

You are creeping beautifully and soon you will be crawling and having fun. This will be easy for you." I found this reassuring and fulfilling to know that I could work with her unconscious (both sub- and superconscious) and empower her to faster development. I was always one step ahead of her development. Amazingly, she walked at eighteen months and developed much faster than the other Down syndrome children in our lives and in her infant stimulation class. Part of this can be attributed to her mosaic diagnosis. There are extreme differences between children with trisomy 21 and the many variations of mosaic Down syndrome.

These minutes of broadcasting were special times of being in touch with both of our soul energies. As I relive it now to share with you, I remember these moments as tender-loving pauses that aided and strengthened my commitment to help Laurie thrive and prosper. Even later, when I was teaching internationally, I would suspend whatever else I was doing to broadcast to Laurie at her bedtime. I knew that I was communicating with her at the deepest level. Sometimes my head would spin with getting her bedtime correct, though. It was hardest when teaching in Australia, ten thousand miles and fourteen hours away from her.

Marcus Bach, a prolific author and expert on Comparative Religions, was lecturing in Virginia Beach at both the Association for Research and Enlightenment and the Fellowship of the Inner Light during the summer after Laurie was born. Paul Solomon had extolled his wisdom and charity. Paul's students had read and were enamored of the book *Jonathan Livingston Seagull*, by Marcus' nephew, Richard Bach. We were excited to meet Marcus.

Paul and Marcus both frequented conferences of spiritual concepts and expanded human potential as presenters. They enjoyed a personal long-distance friendship. Paul told us that Marcus was adept at quickly getting an audience in the palm of his hand. Marcus created a receptive energy within a room in moments with his sincerity. He humbled himself by using self-deprecating humor to build an atmosphere of trust with the audience. Paul suggested that the ILC guides attend his lecture and observe his technique and use of humor. Marcus was a master at making himself vulnerable and endearing to his audiences before presenting his wisdom. He often shared with audiences that he began each morning by crawling. He crawled to the bathroom, to the kitchen, and more. Audiences laughed in disbelief about this 73 year old, dignified author crawling to the bathroom each morning. He convinced them he was serious and explained the importance of crawling—it cross-patterns the brain for increased learning. It keeps both sides of the brain active. He was a proponent of superlearning.

Marcus noticed Laurie in the midst of gatherings. He asked for a meeting with Paul and me. He told us about an organization in Philadelphia that offered cross-patterning work with both special needs and gifted children. He suggested that Laurie be enrolled in The Institutes for the Achievement of Human Potential (The Institute). They had spectacular results. Amazingly, I managed to enroll Laurie in The Institute immediately. Her first visit was set for a week in October when Laurie would be seven months of age. Our church sponsored Laurie. Because I was required to bring a partner or a friend who would assist my learning, another mother with a bright baby Laurie's age joined me.

At The Institute, the children are watched, tested, and observed separately while the parents are instructed. The parents are taught superlearning skills. For five days, we adults wrapped ourselves in blankets to keep from shivering and to survive sitting passively as students in the cold lecture hall. The temperature was a constant 50 degrees. Dr. Glenn Doman explained that this was the best temperature for absorbing knowledge. He elaborated all of the great artistic and cultural capitals of the world had a mean temperature of 50 degrees.

It certainly kept me alert! All participants were relieved that there were ten-minute orange juice and coffee breaks precisely every hour in a 70-degree room. I benefited from this learning environment. Years later in office settings, I gratefully applied a five-minute break on the hour to move and to relieve tension.

The Institute was not a democracy. It was an autocracy, and I agreed to the terms. I came home with a dictate to have three volunteers for each and every day to administer the program. The most dramatic point of the program was the patterning. It was an overwhelming prospect to do this. A child or baby needed three adults to move his or her body in a creeping or crawling movement five times an hour for five minutes, three hours a day. One would move the head and the other two adults would move the legs in the appropriate manner. Suddenly I was a teacher of superlearning to many volunteers, I was a manager of volunteers, and I was a creator of Laurie's curriculum. (The Appendix, "Tools for Empowered Development" contains a deeper explanation of the entire program.)

When we returned home, Laurie charmed her volunteers and gave numerous hugs and kisses after each patterning session. Everyone enjoyed the excitement of watching Laurie make progress. In between body patterning, there were word activities, photo journalistic lessons, and quantity activities. Mostly stay-at-home-moms volunteered. I am still amazed and grateful that volunteers found substitutes who jumped in when they or a child were sick. They stayed on the schedule for months at a time, arranging their own babysitting as necessary. Laurie was most happy when a man showed up on a team. She has always enjoyed men more than women.

Both Laurie and I hated one part of the program. A plastic mask with a small tube was to be placed over a child's face for a minute. When the mask was removed, the child gasped for breath, supposedly increasing the lung capacity. I did not teach many of Laurie's volunteers to do this. If it was done, I supervised it. I always felt unsure about using the mask. I felt cruel when perpetrating it on Laurie, and I always worried about the danger of suffocating her. Many days, I skipped it all together. I stopped it on the day at sixteen months when Laurie grabbed a dowel from her breathing vest and slugged me with it. I agreed with her, that was enough! In fact, it was more than enough!

The Institute demanded 100% cooperation and involvement. You can imagine that this was not easy. On our third trip to The Institutes for the Achievement of Human Potential, Laurie was tested again. She made more progress than all the other children in the project. I was as proud as any parent with the honor student stickers on their cars! She had learned the following:

1. to crawl,
2. to read,
3. to walk, and
4. to make greater social contact.

But I confessed to The Institute that we were not able to do the program 100%. Revealing our truth definitely did not work. Laurie instantly lost her place in the program. Needless to say, I was disappointed. On the other hand, I had learned the process. Because I was employed again as a family and group therapist with a total of two weeks of vacation a year, the trips every six months back and forth to The Institute felt unnecessary. I am sure that additional participation at The Institute would have become burdensome. I continued the program intensely for the next year. Laurie always delighted in being the star of "her show" for two or more hours a day. Volunteers loved receiving her unconditional love with both shared laughter and occasional tears when Laurie became tired. The effort that everyone put into this program was rewarding. Laurie was nearly on schedule with her development until age three.

As we moved around and as I taught internationally, I managed to keep up with portions of the program. In Oslo, we were lucky. We joined with another family doing the program from The Institute. Laurie was thirteen years old. Their home bordered the exquisitely designed Vigeland Park. The youngsters did cross-crawling activities in the beautiful park in good weather and in the family's large recreation room when there was snow on the ground. Laurie and I both enjoyed our daily walks past the world-famous statuary as we returned home diagonally across the park.

When Laurie was three, I was consolidating and repacking some of her educational tools in an attic. She was playing on the floor beside me. I was totally into my task and not thinking about her. I had brought ample toys to amuse her. It did not dawn on me to show her the words. I pulled out one reading word card upside down. As I was putting it back in the box neatly, Laurie said, "Clown." I looked at the word and, sure enough, it was clown. She had not seen this word for over a year. I was overjoyed and relieved to actually hear her say one of the words aloud. We then took a little break, and she obviously enjoyed seeing some of her past lessons. The Institute advised words to be written in red on individual cards. They are presented with joy at a fast pace in varying spaces around the presenter. She did not pronounce all of the words; however, she looked at the correct word when I gave her two choices. This was confirmation that she had learned to read starting at seven months and had retained that knowledge.

I am grateful to Marcus Bach for introducing me to the program, to Paul Solomon for supporting Laurie's program, to The Institute for their efforts, and to all of the people who volunteered to work with Laurie. Thirty years later, Susanna McIlwaine and I became friends in Washington, DC. We discovered that we had lived at the beach at the same time. After two years of friendship, I mentioned that Laurie was patterned by friends while we lived in Virginia Beach and Newport News. "Oh, I knew about Laurie! So, she was the adorable Down syndrome girl everyone was talking about." Laurie and her special healing program were famous.

One frustrating peculiarity about teaching Laurie was that she expected to do things perfectly the first time she attempted a new skill. This personal expectation thwarts an above-average child and is especially bothersome for a cognitively impaired child. Of course, she cut bananas quite perfectly on the first attempt and she tore salad greens perfectly on her first attempt. But holding a pencil or a crayon that slipped out of her grip was a challenging task. Writing the letters of the alphabet perfectly was a challenging task. This need in her for perfection was obviously upsetting for her and stymieing for me. I ended up thinking many times, "My God, she must have been brilliant in her last life time, if she expects to perform tasks perfectly on the first attempt." She was often resistant to trying a new skill a second or third time. She needed much encouragement and, sometimes, a break of a day or two to come back to the task at hand. Through the years, I have needed to say to her, "Laurie, everyone makes mistakes learning new things. I make mistakes all the time even when I know how to do something." I would point out to her when I made errors and needed to erase letters or words. I hoped that this would help her to understand that everyone makes mistakes and would encourage her to accept that it was a normal part of development to make mistakes. Over and over, Laurie seemed in need of receiving the message that if she erred, she was fine.

When Laurie was enrolled in school in the Netherlands, the school curriculum introduced eight words in a twelve-week session. I felt so sorry for Laurie. In The Institute's program, five new words were introduced every day, including weekend days! I am quite sure that she learned the Dutch words within the first two days. Yet she smilingly tolerated the sweet, compassionate teacher-nun. She was also learning to write for the first time and to read out loud. She found that exciting. She enjoyed hugging and kissing the other kids in the class. So, she tolerated being taught only eight new words in twelve weeks. She loved her classmates, busmates, teachers, and the principal. However, I knew that she was not being challenged beyond learning a new language and culture. I continued to teach her five new English words at home each day.

I was not always allowed to provide the best education for Laurie. I asked Dutch school officials if I could enroll Laurie in a school for children with dull-normal intelligence rather than severe incapacity. We were allowed an interview. The elegant modern school was literally nestled in the middle of the dunes on the Scheveningen Beach side of The Hague. It was the loveliest setting that I have ever seen for a school. At that time in her life, Laurie was always excited about seeing new places and meeting new people. As we went through the interview, she was at her best and most charming. Laurie met the new children with delight. After observation and much questioning, I was convinced Laurie was at the exact developmental stage as other children in the respective class. Yet, a week later by letter, I was informed that Laurie could not transfer there. Two years later, I learned that the school never accepted Down syndrome children. The school believed Down syndrome kids could not function at a higher level. There had been no discussion of Laurie's specific mosaic chromosome diagnosis (which includes approximately five percent of Down syndrome children). I was disappointed. I trusted that Laurie was being put where God wanted her.

6 The Mini-Master

"Don't ever restrict Laurie from doing her work!"

~Paul Solomon

While we still lived in Newport News in 1978, a fundamentalist minister stopped me on the street. Normally we talked in his shop, Agape, that was beneath our apartment. He said, "You know this child (of yours) is no accident. God had to send her to you to get you on the right path and to keep you on the right path, on God's path." I nodded and told him that I felt that, too. I remembered Barbara Lesnovitch's psychic message, "You are an angel of God, and don't you forget it!" I chose not to share this other psychic message, which I imagined he might disparage. I thanked him for his "gift of the spirit" and assured him that I would remember.

About this same time, Paul Solomon, my spiritual mentor, invited me to co-teach an ILC weekend class to Virginia Satir, my family therapist mentor, and her colleagues. Paul knew that it was a rare opportunity for me. Virginia is considered the mother of family therapy. She traveled the world to teach mental health professionals, and her books were translated into several languages. For this workshop, she had invited renowned leaders in family therapy from around the country who were her closest friends to take this class in spiritual development in Chevy Chase, Maryland. I was very excited to see Virginia again as well as to see old friends from the Satir Network. I drove up with Paul from Virginia Beach. When we arrived, it was heartwarming to see and hug old friends whom I had met during lengthy Satir workshops or Satir network reunions in Minnesota, Florida, Aruba, and Mexico.

It was an exciting weekend for me. It was thrilling to assist one mentor give a class to another mentor. The weekend felt like an initiation for me. The audience was not the easiest! The participants were dynamic national leaders in psychology and psychiatry. They normally presented information to large audiences. Possibly they were not as receptive for spiritual development as Virginia thought they were. To say they were "full of themselves" is an understatement. These were people who did bow to Virginia's wisdom. However, most of them fought Paul's lectures the entire weekend. They accepted me as an assistant and cooperated when I led meditations and experiential exercises. We only finished two thirds of the normal weekend's agenda because they interrupted Paul so often.

On Monday morning, I took Paul to the airport as he flew off to Alaska and Japan on a teaching tour. I proceeded to drive his new maroon Cadillac back to Virginia Beach. It was mid-morning; the roads were empty, the weather was beautiful, and the automatic cruise control was a Godsend.

At Sufi camp I had learned a mantra for forgiveness, Ya Ghaffar. It is one of the Ninety-Nine Names of God in the Muslim tradition. I was fond of using it, and it was part of my repertoire of chants and mantras. It is considered the name of "He Who Is All Forgiving." It is written that the one repeating this name will be forgiven his/her sins. Driving back from this rare opportunity in Washington, DC, I used the mantra and found a fountain of forgiveness. The Ya Ghaffar mantra began unbidden in my subconscious. I found it interesting and began to work with it. I thought, "What do I want to forgive myself for?"

I forgave myself for not having a long-term relationship and for being an unwed mother. I forgave Laurie for wanting to experience an incomplete family life. I forgave her for coming in without a willing father. I thanked Laurie for choosing me. I forgave Laurie for choosing a father that did not want to be involved with us. Forgiving Laurie for choosing to come into this lifetime outside of marriage was very cleansing for me and felt empowering. In some way, this aspect of the forgiveness brought us to a kind of equality. I began sobbing as the mantra was automatically resonating deeply inside me. When the sobbing abated, I continued to repeat it aloud.

I continued to use the mantra and thought I should work at forgiving Saul. I forgave myself for getting pregnant in a one-night stand. I forgave myself for committing adultery and asked God to forgive me for that. I asked Saul's wife, soul-to-soul, to forgive me for sleeping with her husband. I forgave myself for feeling that I needed to stay out of the Sufi Order, for believing there was not room for the two of us and this big secret. I forgave Saul for ignoring my letter. I forgave him for not recognizing us. I forgave him for his lack of involvement.

This unscheduled ritual had gone on for over an hour. Both the car and I seemed to be on cruise control. I forgave Saul again for not acknowledging us and then… it was if a shower of light rays began to flow in through the crown of my head. I realized I was in a shimmering Fountain of Forgiveness. This must have continued intensely for ten or so minutes. This was the first time and blessedly not the last time, that I experienced real forgiveness, not empty words. It is actually a feeling and an emotion of purification. Every cell in my body felt vibrant, energized, and cleansed as Route 64 led me back home.

As mentioned earlier, Laurie and I moved in 1979 to Carmel in the Valley, a New Age community in Timberville, Virginia, that the Fellowship was creating. We opened the community with a large healing conference. Among the famous guests and speakers were Buckminster Fuller, Pir Vilayat Inayat Khan, Sir George Trevelyan, and Elizabeth Kubler-Ross. On the early Sunday morning session, all conference participants were gathered outdoors. Laurie and I were in the front row with the other mothers, toddlers, and babies. The honored guests were standing in front facing the audience. Laurie was itching to join them. She kept trying to wiggle out of my grasp. I tried to hold on to her without creating a scene. Finally, Paul shot a scolding glare at me that let me know I should just let her go. She ran to the group and jumped into Sir George Trevelyan's waiting arms. They had a smiling, adoring love-fest for several minutes. And everyone in the audience had a heart-warming-chuckling-love-fest as they watched this 73-year-old, elegant English Baronet, New Age leader and the three-year-old cherub in the perfect Polly Flinders dress relish in each other's joy.

The day after the conference, Paul and I had an appointment about my teaching assignments. As I sat down in front of his desk, he said harshly, "Don't ever restrict Laurie from doing her work!" I was puzzled and felt severely reprimanded. I felt my cheeks color. He went on to explain, "You don't know what she has planned. And you don't know what she is doing. Give her more freedom. She knows in her soul what magic she is doing. Do you understand?" He scolded again, "Don't ever restrict Laurie from doing her work!"

This advice created an inner tussle for me. It was not easy to know when to keep Laurie well-behaved and socialized and when to let her do her spiritual work. Normally, I gave her quite free reign to work her magic. I had already experienced many examples of her effects on people in positive ways. Through the years, people reported that Laurie was instructing them in dreams or that she changed their lives after spending a short amount of time with her. When she was an infant, several people at the Fellowship came to me and reported that they had dreams in which they were in a large classroom or auditorium and Laurie was a revered teacher.

The Mini-Master

They reported that she appeared either as a baby or a child. They were in awe of her and understood that there was more than a Down syndrome, drooling baby in front of them. With Paul's admonition, these memories of Laurie's ability to teach in large groups became prophesies and not "just dreams." I was again reminded: I am the guardian of a master teacher.

For years I was convinced, and so were others, that people who spent time in Laurie's presence had their lives changed for the better. Actually, I believe this is as true today as it was earlier. It was as if caring for her gave a person more merit, more courage, and more fortitude to carry on what they needed to do. When she was four years old and in spiritual community, the students called Laurie the "Mini-Master." On a daily basis she presented people with the hardest lessons they were approaching in their journals, prayers, and meditations! Now, I know other children also do this. In fact, I believe everyone in our lives is there to teach us the Divine lessons we need to learn.

However, my fellow community members assured me that their lessons were more extreme with Laurie—better or worse depending on their frame of mind. She offered intense lessons in patience, compassion, understanding, vigilance, anger management, clarity, joyfulness, gentleness, balance, creativity, and facing life with knowledge of The Divine Comedy. People were either reluctant to spend a day with Laurie or excited depending upon their willingness to have their karmic lessons splattered in their face with sticky little fingers and an impish grin! The sparkling humor emanating from Laurie's eyes helped you realize that she was testing you in love and respect and not from spite or a power struggle. If you plugged into "right action" and managed a wise response, fun, hugs, and peace ensued. Often Laurie would end the scene by holding her adult student's face between her hot healing hands and by then planting a kiss on the nose, the forehead, or the mouth as if to say, "Well done!"

One of our neighbors, a kindly, devoted Christian woman, often babysat for Laurie when the au pair and I attended the evening classes at Hearthfire Lodge together. One day as I dropped Laurie off, we had tea together. Dale shared that her knee had been aching terribly for a week. Laurie, age four, knelt on the floor, rubbed the knee gently, and kissed it several times. The next day the neighbor exclaimed in surprise, "You know, Laurie healed my knee. She actually healed my knee! It feels perfect now."

I was not surprised and nodded. "She knows how to work with God. To tell you the truth, I am more surprised when Laurie does not heal a situation than I am when she does."

Paul Solomon defined perfect health as "having the exact symptoms needed to learn a lesson or accomplish a goal." Basically that means that we are all always in perfect health and, if ill, we have a soul lesson to learn. Hopefully, we learn our lessons well and accomplish our goals. Laurie's Down syndrome diagnosis is a perfect means for her to accomplish her goal.

Several people in the States, the Netherlands, and Norway have chosen special education degrees after spending a few days, a weekend, or just an hour or two with Laurie. One babysitter was transformed by her encounter with Laurie. She was a young, thirty-something woman who had not yet settled on a career. She shared with me that she had been wafting back and forth and trying to decide on a life path. She babysat Laurie during two weeks while I was teaching in the evenings. The following week, she re-enrolled in school to finish her degree. She changed her major to special education. She graduated quickly and was delighted with her new career. She found me on the internet recently after 32 years. My heart and soul felt so touched by her message:

"I have thought of you and Laurie Shanti often and wondered how you are…I'm alive and well…and still work with children and adults with challenges in the community to help with cognitive gains and independent living skills."

Most au pairs and babysitters have been transformed within weeks or months of spending time with Laurie. They have finished degrees they had been ignoring or struggling with for years. They have found endearing and enduring relationships. (Believe me, I have often wondered why she hasn't had that affect on me—although I know she has been jealous of my suitors.) They find great jobs. It is as if Laurie elevates their lives. They have offered rich experiences to her also. They have taught her to read from books in three languages, to bike down mountains in Oslo, to cook new and exciting foods, to look at life from many angles. They offered a wide variety of experiences that I did not and could not offer Laurie. From the time she was three until she was 21, we generally were apart 50% of the year. Laurie has been enriched by my having been on the road so many weeks at a time during her lifetime. I missed her terribly, yet felt blessed to know that we were both doing our spiritual light work.

Starting at age three, Laurie would often say in a typical Aries attitude, "I'm the boss!" And I would quietly state, "No, I am the boss of the family." Usually the discussion ended when I would say firmly, "This lifetime, I'm the parent and you are a child. I'm the boss now." When she was four and I was about to leave on a six-week teaching trip, she had a new au pair. The night before I was to leave, we gathered in the kitchen. I said to Laurie, "I am the big boss and Patricia is the second boss. You are to listen to her and cooperate with her." I asked her if she understood. Laurie nodded, looked up at us with arms akimbo and boasted decisively, "Yes, and I'm the little boss!"

I still cannot tell that story without seeing her determined face and without laughing proudly of her inherent strength. Patricia and I agreed with her that she was indeed the little boss and still made sure that she understood the family pecking order.

One of my favorite stories about Laurie's masterful teaching at a young age was told to me when Laurie was fourteen. In 1990, Doug, a North Carolina pharmacist, reported a story that he thought happened in 1980. Laurie would have been four years old. At a church picnic, she found him sitting alone in a corner of the church yard, despondent and sniffling. He explained to me that he had been heartbroken over a failed relationship. Laurie crawled into his lap, hugged him and kissed him, and then a few minutes later took him by the hand. She led him to a car. They sat in the car and she sat in his lap and encouraged him to cry. He grieved and relaxed. Then she reached down to find a thermos and offered him a drink. It was lemonade. He felt consoled, comforted, and relieved to receive her caring. They got out of the car and joined the other parishioners at the church yard picnic. But as they were walking away, Doug noticed that an unknown family got into the car, obviously their car, and drove off! He was sure that Laurie and he had been comfortably secluded in my car. We each roared with laughter at Laurie's immediacy to find an appropriate car-office to do her healing work. He assured me that Laurie's love and comforting, wordless understanding had blessed him those ten years.

Just recently, one of the former Dutch babysitters found me on the Peace Through Understanding Web site. She was relieved to find us, she said. She had been feeling the need to thank me for how much her life had been changed by my influence in her life twenty-four years ago. She said that she recognized how more spiritual her life became after babysitting Laurie. She gave me credit even though she never took a workshop or attended a lecture with me. I assured her that it was not me who had influenced and elevated her life; it was nine-year-old Laurie.

Dielly Bartels recently shared with me how Laurie affected her one evening in my apartment in Holland. It was in August 1986, and Laurie was ten. Earlier in the year, Dielly had cared for Laurie in February/March and afterward had missed her terribly. That longing increased after spending another month with Laurie in June/July. Caring for Laurie awoke her deep longing to be a mother. Dielly is one of the people who found their life partner within weeks of babysitting Laurie. She was in a new relationship with the man who would later become her husband and who was not ready for parenthood at that time. That day in the workshop that I led, Dielly experienced past life memories of troubled motherhoods, either of having no child or of being a stressed single mother. Dielly then shared how deeply she wanted a child this lifetime. As the sentence ended, Laurie, who appeared to be sleep walking, came out of her room, headed straight to Dielly, and nestled into her lap. Laurie slept there as if she was Dielly's child. As I think of the story now, it was as if in those moments there was a soul fostering of Laurie to Dielly. Dielly is one of the people who has recognized Laurie as a "child of man," as Paul's reading in 1977 suggested. Dielly remains a second mother figure for Laurie and a figure of a dear younger sister to me.

When Laurie was nine, I was often furious, because she tested my limits every day, all day! I had grown so tired of the testing that I sadly had stopped setting limits some days. Finally a school teacher said to me, "This is what special needs kids do, they continually test the limits. It will always happen. You will always have to set limits." I then waited daily for the test with the alertness of a lioness lying in wait for prey to appear. I began to think of it as a daily ritual. She would test me. I would reset the limits. I vowed to myself that I would reset the boundaries immediately and firmly each time. Even though I had been resistant to establishing boundaries, I learned to do it. Things got better. A few years later, I realized that daily testing had generally stopped. The Mini-Master had successfully taught her loosey-goosey mother structure.

Our family boundaries were always tested when I came back from long teaching tours. When we were reunited after a lengthy absence, there would be ten minutes of bashful hugs and quick kisses, then the melding hugs and longer kisses would come with some show and tell time, tickles, giggles, and exchanging of tokens. The normal energy between us returned quickly and Laurie would test our established limits within a half hour. After each trip, I needed to firmly declare that I was back and that the rules were the same as before I left. She'd exhibit some kind of an "Oh, darn!" attitude and strut off. Then life proceeded as normal.

In mid-April 1985, I received a letter from two directors of growth centers in Oslo, Norway. They invited me to teach a workshop for them in the autumn. I accepted and immediately thought it would be a wonderful opportunity to do my work in Oslo for nine days, meet new people, and get a classic Norwegian sweater. This was one of my little-did-I-know moments. I never could have imagined that nearly half of those participants from this first workshop in Norway would become valued friends and colleagues. Three of the women would become dear soul-sisters to me. Nor did I imagine that, while I would be teaching the workshop entitled "Overcoming Your Karma with Joy, Laughter and Tears," the Mini-Master, now age nine, would be giving an intensive on "Self-Assertion and Princely Qualities."

The center directors accepted my workshop proposal and asked if I would also do private sessions. I offered to do three-hour-long Wellsprings Massage sessions. I explained that the massage offered an opportunity to bring up past life memories and to release stress out of the body, mind, and spirit. I asked that the potential clients be known to them and that they could assure me the clients possessed sound mental health. They agreed. I explained that my daughter, diagnosed as Down syndrome, would accompany me. I asked if they thought they could arrange child care. They assured me they would take care of child care. They explained that we would be living in the Solverv Center in Oslo, where I would be giving sessions. I looked forward to the trip and thought Laurie and I would have a "nice little autumnal vacation."

When we arrived, I discovered that my workshop was packed with eager participants. What surprised me more was that my schedule for the nine days was totally booked except for three blocks of time. Norwegians were hungry for the opportunity to do past life work. I had Friday afternoon off to unpack, to get Laurie oriented, and to prepare for the Friday evening through Sunday workshop. Sunday night was free for dinner after the workshop and Thursday evening was free. Other than that, I was booked morning, noon, and night for nine days. I thought, "Oh, poor Laurie, may her child care be perfect!" And I wondered how I would survive while giving so many intense sessions in so few days.

Hans Jacob volunteered to watch Laurie. He was in residence at Solverv for several weeks doing intensive studies in self-realization, taking art classes, and attending concerts and lectures about town. Solverv rented rooms inexpensively to alternative lifestyle people interested in modern psychology. Residents came in from all areas of Norway, including isolated villages and islands. The atmosphere was warm and inviting. The white wooden building had been a tuberculosis sanitarium for young girls earlier in the twentieth century. The architecture was quaint, the floors were slanted, and no matter how much paint was used, it still looked run down. It was a twenty-minute tram ride up the hill from Oslo's market square.

Hans Jacob was a handsome, gentle-yet-towering, and unassuming retired engineer who lived above the Arctic Circle. His English was impeccable. Hans Jacob had used English daily during his long career of engineering in many different countries on several continents. He shared that he would soon return home to the far north to be hunkered down for the long dark winter on a small, sparsely inhabited island that his family owned. This fortunate family had a large fishing company that supplied masses of cod stock fish (bacalao) to Spain and Portugal. I discovered later that they also owned the local ferries, several islands, and most of the shops and services on those islands.

Laurie crawled into Hans Jacob's lap immediately, and they were friends from the start. After the first evening, he mentioned with surprise how strong-willed she was. I apologized for not warning him. With a grin, I suggested that he set limits immediately to ensure his survival. He looked relieved. When he realized that he wouldn't damage her psyche by setting boundaries of behavior, he knew he could manage Laurie. He laughed, explaining that he had supervised many young engineers in foreign countries. He would use those skills to work with Laurie.

Hans Jacob had just finished a special drawing class in the previous week and had many colorful supplies that he brought to the kitchen table at the center. Laurie enjoyed the free-form expression he evoked from her. They created swirls of undefined shapes in many colors. They read and re-read the many books we had brought. They took walks, cuddled, and talked. She re-taught him many fairy tales and insisted that they act them out several times each day. She played the princess, of course, and the female antagonist roles. He filled in the other roles. He laughed several times during the week, sharing that "Laurie doesn't think I'm a very good prince. She keeps trying to teach me how to be a prince. And I hope you don't mind, she is calling me "Opa." Opa is the Dutch word for grandfather.

I assured him that it was fine. "She has one grandfather and she only gets to see him for a few days every other year. It is wonderful she loves you so much and sees you as a grandfather."

During breakfast and our tea breaks together, I realized Hans Jacob was one of the noblest, best-read, respectful, open-minded, grounded, and flexible men I had ever met. He was modest and did not seem to have more than a stitch of charisma. Laurie expected princes in "her" fairy tales to be gallant and charismatic. Hans Jacob was definitely lacking in these qualities. Laurie kept demonstrating princely qualities. Hans Jacob kept failing to meet her standard. Laurie kept coaching. Hans Jacob kept working at finding his prince within. Hans Jacob unexpectedly found himself enrolled in the Mini-Master's nine-day-course of "Self-Assertion and Princely Qualities." When we left Oslo, I felt blessed that Laurie had been in his care. When we returned home to the Netherlands, Laurie missed Hans Jacob. She often mentioned him.

Norwegians continued to be interested in my work. Lois Reirsøl, the director of Sølverv, kept inviting me back to do workshops and sessions five times a year. I normally stayed for a month at a time. During one of the ski-week vacations in the Netherlands, I flew Laurie and her au pair up to Norway for a week's vacation. We were delighted to find that Hans Jacob was down from the north escaping the polar night. My dear soul-sister, Gerd Bjorke, was putting us up and agreed that we could give a Valentine's dinner for her and Hans Jacob. Laurie was delighted to snuggle and hug her Opa.

That evening Hans Jacob explained that he valued those days he had spent with Laurie two years earlier. He believed they had been some of the most important days in his life on his quest of self-realization. He shared that he continued to work with her coaching and the guidance she imparted during those nine days. Smilingly, he reported that his wife was grateful to Laurie. "Laurie taught me how to be a prince. It's never too late to learn to be a prince."

Hans Jacob offered, "When you have time, you must come north and visit my wife and me. Come see the midnight sun. We would like that very much." I assured him that it would happen.

Lois offered me a full-time position several times. I finally agreed. We moved to Oslo on February 7, 1989. During our first June as Norwegian residents, I accepted an offer to help a retired ailing client with her annual drive north above the Arctic Circle. She spent summers at her family's homestead and liked to have company to share the long drive. She suggested that we could take our time and sightsee a bit on the way north. It was a wonderful invitation to enjoy her delightful company and the beautiful topography. Laurie and I would have the opportunity to experience the midnight sun on Hans Jacob's family's island above the Arctic Circle and to meet his wife.

Laurie loved the idea of traveling to see her Opa and was excited from day one of the trip. The further north we drove, the more she expressed dislike of our driving through lush spring green valleys with dark, rock-surfaced mountains on every side. I knew she had depth perception difficulties and disliked walking on steep terrain. I was very careful with helping her over rocks and hills, typical Norwegian topography. I did not know at the time that she had undiagnosed astigmatism, which was the reason that walking on rocks and hills was so difficult. I, on the other hand, enjoyed the trip. Much of the snow had melted away by mid-June. I kept a daily count of snow-fed waterfalls and enjoyed our trip through vast valleys and tunnels of varying ages, colors and sizes. We enjoyed brief romps on beaches of many different colored sands and textures around the fjords. We both enjoyed the numerous ferry rides. On the chilly and misty ferry ride to the rugged island of Lofoton, Laurie flirted charmingly with the captain. This got us invited into the sleekly modern, warm and toasty captain's deck.

Norway has one of the highest costs of living in the world. We decided that one way we could economize was to pack picnic lunches. The picnic tables at rest stops seemed to always be perched on top of rocky mounds perfect for native Norwegians, reindeer, moose, and/or mountain goats. Laurie was disgusted with the terrain. Twice in tears, she insisted she be allowed to eat in the car. To please her, we would stop for an afternoon treat in a café with a flat parking lot. Laurie was relieved to find that Hans Jacob's small harbor and neighborhood of fifteen or so homes was relatively flat. She refused the invitation to walk on the rocky shoreline to see masses of nesting sea birds. She was satisfied that she had seen seagull chicks from flat sea-level walkways on Lofoten where we had vacationed for two days.

As we left his island, Hans Jacob drove us to the neighboring island of Skjervøy. Its name actually translates as "island of rocky ground." We visited a small Sami Center there and started our journey home by boarding the Hurtigruten, a large ferry that transports people, products and cars up and down the Norwegian Coast. Laurie breathed a sigh of relief when she stepped onto the polished flat deck of the shiplike ferry. It was obvious that she was happy to be on a flat surface. She understood that we were on our way back south. I explained that we were "three sleeps" from being home. We would sleep on the boat one night, visit the most famous church in Norway, sleep two nights in a Trondheim hotel, and then take a long train ride home. She smiled and was happy that the trip would soon be over. We went to bed early. The Hurtigruten hugs the coastline. So when we awoke in the morning, the view of the coast was perfectly clear from our breakfast table. Laurie looked up and out and in disgust shouted, "Oh, no! Not more mountains!" She was delighted when we returned home to our neighborhood in Oslo, which was nearly at sea level.

During the summer school of 1989, our beloved friend and the "symbols man" of Peace Through Understanding, Jan Ton, came to me and said, "I can't believe Laurie!" He went on to exclaim: "She's put me through a different test every day this year in summer school. She wants to eat lunch with me and then she acts differently toward me every day. She is recapping all of my lessons in relationships with women. She's reenacted communication challenges I have had with old lovers this entire week!" Jan was wise enough to see it and knew he was being set up and taught. The Mini-Master was giving the Mystery School symbols teacher a relationship review. Jan was wise enough to honor the teaching. Following is his recent sharing on how the "daily plays" with Laurie ultimately affected his relationship with his wife, Gerry:

The summer school in Belgium, when Laurie was mirroring my female counterparts, is often on my mind. Gerry and I knew each other then for almost a year and we were still in the hesitating, exploring phase.

In the silent hours of those summer days I wrote a long letter to Gerry. Thanks to Laurie, I could express very openly and clearly how I saw our relationship. I found a beautiful balance between openness and firmness, between allowing freedom and free choice and on other hand I was very clear about my limits and what I didn't want. The letter was so penetrating, that Gerry needed several weeks before she could respond. When we met again, the doors between our hearts and minds opened wide. ... Sometimes we read the letter again and it is always a source of inspiration.

The daily plays with Laurie were the basis for the tone I found in writing that letter. The hardest thing was that she was constantly following me and asking for attention. That in itself is one of my most allergic spots. I learned to protect my space, to be clear about my limits. And most of all to realize during the hardest parts, that I still loved her and she loved me.

I am aware that students and staff members of the four-week summer retreats were as affected by Laurie's teachings as they were by the extraordinary staff members I was lucky enough to gather.

When we moved to Oslo, I was engaged to be engaged. Two months after we established residency, Fritjof (name changed) came over one night looking very serious. He had spent three hours alone with Laurie the day before. He said to me, "Laurie sees right through me, and I can't take it. There is no way I can live with you and Laurie. There can be no future together. We must break up." He shared that he always considered himself the great liberal and now considered himself limited in being able to accept Laurie. He uncharacteristically sobbed several times and shared that he was very disappointed in himself. He apologized and left. I was in shock.

My immediate thoughts were, "I am so grateful for Laurie's ability to see right through me. It is a gift. I love her honesty. I am secure in her honesty." Yet for a month I was furious and heartsick that I had moved into the northern darkness of Norway for this relationship that was now ended. Fortunately, I realized again that Laurie knew what she was doing. I trusted that God had found a way to move me into an appropriate place of service. I understood that there had to be other reasons, not so obvious to me then, for us to have moved north. Laurie became enrolled in a Rudolf Steiner School, which embraced and enhanced her creative nature. Soon, counseling and teaching at Sølverv in Norway and the students of Peace Through Understanding in the Netherlands became my focus. I was no longer distracted by the lost relationship.

While residing in Norway, it was easier to pursue my Buddhist studies in the Netherlands on teaching tours. Public transportation was better in the Netherlands, and Laurie was generally with an au pair in Norway. Plus, the sangha (congregation) in the Netherlands felt like family to us and always welcomed us warmly. One school holiday, Laurie came with me to visit a past au pair and her new husband in The Hague. I went to the east of the country for a Buddhist training for the week. Laurie was fourteen. The morning after I arrived at the center, Farida, Laurie's hostess, called and said, "Laurie is acting like a monster with my husband. I have never seen her like this. I cannot get her to change her behavior. I have to get her out of the house. My husband is threatening to leave! Can I bring her to you?"

I laughed knowingly and a bit too smugly. "Obviously, Laurie needs to be here. Please bring her." I instantly thought that Laurie needed to be in a holy atmosphere and in the presence of the teacher. Little did I know I would discover years later that one of my fellow Buddhist students had a cosmic date with Laurie. And, even over my careful planning of her vacation and life, Laurie had found a way to keep her appointment!

Shortly after Laurie was brought to the center, she latched on to a handsome hunk named Wim in his late twenties. She would not let him out of her sight. Generally she did not come into the teaching room. She was content re-reading her books, doing jigsaw puzzles on her own in the common room, or helping in the kitchen.

During free time she followed Wim everywhere. I was amused, knowing that she was doing her holy work. I did not curtail her. She declared her love for him, asked him to marry her, staged pretend wedding ceremonies, and curled up in his lap as much as possible. Wim was beside himself. He has a warm, gentle inclusive personality with the welcoming smile almost always on the face of dedicated students of Tibetan Buddhism. He is endearing and he did not know how to handle Laurie's abundant and rather conditional attention. He did not want to hurt her or mislead her. He asked me for help. I shared that she was raised with directness and transparency. So he could tell her when it was too much and when he needed space. I assured him that she would do the same to him if the tables were turned. He asked her for more space. It helped some.

Being a sensitive and aware being, Wim knew that Laurie was teaching him. He shared that he had just broken up with a girlfriend and was hoping to meet someone special soon. He had a fear of being obsessed over. Laurie was triggering that trepidation. Laurie's attention was forcing him to face his intimacy challenges over and over each day of the retreat.

Many years later, we returned to the Netherlands for a Dagpo Rinpoche Buddhist seminar. Wim was there. As soon as he spotted us, he enthusiastically rushed over to us. It was obvious that he was pleased to see us again. He hugged Laurie and thanked her for being an inspiration to him. Wim shared that he had married and had several children; one of them was a Down syndrome baby girl. While beaming, Wim credited Laurie for reminding him of a need to prepare for intimacy AND for making it easy to accept his special needs child, whom he calls his "special angel."

We have seen Wim three times since then. Each time, he expresses loving gratitude to Laurie for exposing him to the beauty of unconditional love. By becoming Wim's friend, the Mini-Master opened his heart and mind for fathering his special angel. Usually his family gathers in the training room for Dagpo Rinpoche's blessings during the final session of each workshop. Wim's dedication and appreciation of the honor of fathering a soul wishing to express as a Down syndrome child is heart-warming.

The admonition from Paul that Laurie knows what she is doing was played out one cold evening in Oslo when Laurie was fourteen. Six or seven rowdy boys, most likely fifteen year olds, were rough-housing on a tram platform in the middle of a boulevard. On the sidewalk, two traffic lanes away, I could hear fists smacking arms and backs through thick parkas. It was dark but probably not later than 8:00 p.m. on a school night. They were yelling aggressively at each other. Two boys seemed to be getting the worst of the bullying, appropriately called "mobbing" in Norway. There were no adults on the platform. Laurie and I were on the sidewalk waiting for a bus. She wanted desperately to cross over to the platform and say hi to the boys. I did not want to teach her that it was okay to approach a group of boys acting violently with each other. She was insistent. Reluctantly, I gave her permission to cross the street to the platform. After all, I was observing.

Laurie did not know the boys. I was unsure how they would respond to her as a special needs person. I was afraid that they would reject her or—worse—"mob" her by taunting her. She joined them on the platform. She said, "Hello" in English rather than "Hei" in Norwegian. The leader stopped punching his victim, turned, smiled and graciously said, "Hello." The boys immediately calmed down and turned receptively to her.

She said, "I'm Laurie and I want to meet you." They each introduced themselves to her by first name. Their tone was gentle and amazingly polite. They talked with her in English for about three minutes. Then Laurie explained she needed to cross the street to catch a bus with her mother. She said, "Bye, bye," turned, and walked away.

In unison, they respectfully turned and cherub-like echoed, "Bye, bye," to her. They waved as she walked away.

I cried as she crossed the street, not understanding how she had done what she had done. As I see this now in my mind's eye, these boys emanated the purity of seven year olds awaiting first communion after Laurie greeted them. The group remained calm and quiet until they boarded their tram. I knew from watching groups of aggressive boys punching each other in many cities and countries that not many people would have had Laurie's effect! Inwardly, I bowed to Laurie and was glad that she had been so persistent to go to them. The Mini-Master created her peaceful victory.

7 Here I Am!

"Be careful lest you entertain angels unaware."

~Hebrews 13:2

When reading *Angel Unaware* as a teenager, my heart swelled with compassion as Dale Evans Rogers, wife of cowboy Roy Rogers, shared the story of the short life of their Down syndrome daughter. I was touched with the beauty and insight of their story. I was raised in rural northern Indiana. I had little experience with this diagnosis, other than being chased around a dining room table at age 16 by a Down syndrome girl while I was selling magazines door-to door. This 14 year old was sheltered at home with no opportunities for socializing or education in the late 1950s. She was so surprised and excited to see me that she screeched with delight and rushed at me. Unfortunately, I was terrified by her response to my visit. That evening my parents explained that her poor farming family had two options for her care—home care or state institutionalization without education. I am sure her family gained merit by offering her a loving home and they gained blessings by receiving her loving tenderness. .

I learned as quickly as I could about Laurie's "condition" and the myths regarding stubbornness and unconditional loving. As mentioned earlier, I was assured that Laurie's lungs and heart were perfect and that she would have a normal life expectancy. The nurses and doctors at the hospital told me immediately to inquire about infant stimulation. I followed up immediately and, as mentioned earlier, Laurie was in school and stimulated from the age of six months. We were lucky. I received helpful information to increase her potential.

When Laurie was an infant, several spiritual leaders/ministers assured me that Laurie was not typical. Many people went out of their way to tell me that I was raising a special daughter. So, I have not been raising or entertaining an "angel unaware." Repeatedly, I was told that I was raising a holy being who was a powerful healer and that I needed to be aware and learn my lessons.

Soon after Laurie's birth, Paul Solomon shared with me that Laurie was a master of healing and could throw powerful energy with her fingers, hands, and thoughts. And goodness knows I have been healed many times by her hands. Paul and another healer used to shoot healing energy back and forth from their finger tips with Laurie before she could walk. I did not understand what they were doing. I am not clairvoyant, so I could not see the sparks flying. However, their smiles and reactive jumps convinced me something exciting and electric was going on between them. Infant Laurie was an equal participant.

When Laurie was just a few weeks old, I was startled when relaxing in bed with her. I kept catching an unwelcome clairvoyant view of a small being that looked like a leprechaun. He had a crooked hat and hung out in the corner of our bedroom ceiling. He was always smiling and seemed to be informally on guard. I wasn't smoking anything and I wasn't hallucinating about anything else. I assumed that I was able to see him because I was so relaxed from meditation and nursing Laurie. I was glad he was there, yet I did not want to be able to see him! I told very few people about her guard and friend and did my best to stay grounded so I could avoid observing him. Now, I suppose I missed an opportunity to talk with him or communicate nonverbally with him. Once in awhile when Laurie was between fourteen and eighteen months old, several of us noticed that she would be in "conversation" with us and then suddenly ignore us. She would look away and seem to be joyously communicating nonverbally with some invisible being her height. Possibly Mr. Crooked Hat stayed around longer than I thought.

Laurie joined me for a summer retreat program in Holland in 1983. This was her first overseas trip. When we fly, my Ms. Aries beloved daughter always gets the window seat. It was an amazingly clear day for the Netherlands and she watched from the window to see the lush green, rectangular fields bordered by grachts (ditches) on the approach. Fields filled with swans and sheep were visible. As soon as the fasten seat belt sign was switched off, she stood up proclaiming proudly and loudly, "My Holland!" She adored life in Holland that summer. Friends taught as a Dutch folk song which translates as: "Holland, My Holland, I find you so fair!" We still enjoy singing it.

The next autumn, when we returned home to the Shenandoah Valley in Virginia, Laurie entered my room morning after morning and said to me, "I go to 'My Holland' and I sleep in a big boat." After a week or so, I found this amusing and irritating. I did my best to explain repeatedly to Laurie there were no more trips planned for her to visit Holland and I knew nothing about a big boat. Little did I know what God was scheduling for our lives. In mid-November, Paul Solomon called me into his office and announced that he had been asked to send a teacher to the Benelux ILC nonprofit for a year. He had chosen me. I accepted the offer. Because I had a tour of Australia and New Zealand planned from New Years to April, I closed our life out quickly in the Valley so that we could establish living arrangements in Europe and Laurie could be taken care of in my absence.

Laurie and I moved to Holland on December 10, 1983, to begin our new venture. Matthew Howard Houston, a dear ILC friend, invited us to his home on the island of Jersey for Christmas. It seemed like a great solution for the holidays since we would not have a home established until the spring. As I made the travel arrangements, I reeled. Laurie was a dream prognosticator. She got to her Holland and she would sleep on a "big boat" not once but twice as we took the overnight ferry to London and back. The Mini-Master was right once again! Even though I taught dream workshops, I started to take my own dream journaling more seriously.

We actually established a home in the spring of 1984 with the help of many kind people, especially Leida Meyer. Leida took us on as a project and helped find a beautiful home that needed a house sitter. I am forever grateful for her loving care and attention to Laurie's needs. Laurie turned eight that spring as we settled in for what I thought was going to be one year in the Netherlands. In fact, our European "tour" turned into fourteen years. We spent five years in the Netherlands and nine years in Norway. For many years I spent half of the time traveling between the two countries. Laurie was always enrolled in a local school, learning the local language and culture.

After arriving in the Netherlands, several people recommended that I have a session and psychic reading with an American Dutchman named Corrie Van Loon. I asked him how I could most effectively handle my hectic schedule teaching at a different venue each week end and still offer stability to Laurie. Corrie told me that Laurie was a master and would *always* take care of herself. I did not really need to worry about her. He had a vision of me being rather Pollyanna-like in a field of daisies and suggested that I reach for maturity.

Here I Am!

I often remember the reading and the message and have been reassured by it many times. Basically, Laurie and I operate within a large extended family (with people of choice) that is spread over two continents and four countries. As mentioned earlier, my mother passed away while I was in college, and my father passed away in 2001. Gene, my half-brother, who is nine years my senior, has always lived eight hundred to six thousand miles away from me for over sixty years. There have been too few visits. His children have settled in the Denver area and one recently moved to Kentucky. Laurie has never met her cousins and would be thrilled to meet them. Even though we have made offers of traveling to them, we have not received any feedback.

There are certainly no expectations or wishes that they will care for Laurie after my demise. I am beginning to make preparation her future, because we have almost no blood family involvement. Yet, I am reassured by Corrie's reading that she can and will "take care of herself."

I was reminded of a message I received in a psychic reading from Paul that was done during an advanced training he called The Forty Days in the Wilderness. This retreat was held in the mountains of West Virginia during the summer of 1977. Laurie was fourteen months old at that time. The reading states Laurie was a "child of man." Paul explained that Laurie belongs to the people and not just to me. This has often puzzled me, and sometimes I have glimpses of what this means. I still believe there is a deeper meaning that has eluded me. Paul reminded me that Jesus is called the son of man in the Bible. Part of my motivation for writing Laurie's story is to give her to the people and not hoard her wisdom and love.

When Laurie was an infant, Tara Singh, yoga teacher and proponent of *The Course of Miracles,* was at The Fellowship for over a year. He told me that Laurie's energy was so pure that she could not tolerate to live on planet Earth past the age of eight. He also told me that her picture should be before the public. This seldom happened. I certainly prayed that he was wrong about her life span, and he was. Sometimes I wonder if I have caused her some impurity that has kept her here longer. I have been very happy Laurie has decided to stay longer. Hopefully, the pictures of Laurie on the cover fulfill Tara's wish.

When she was eight, I had a terrible scare in the Netherlands. I had been in The Hague teaching before we were actually settled in an apartment together. Laurie was staying with a family in the north of the country as I traveled and taught. They called early one morning and said Laurie was being rushed to a hospital, her tongue was so swollen upon awakening that she could barely breathe. They asked me if she was allergic to any medicines. I asked them not to give her penicillin because I am allergic to it, and I reminded them again of her food allergies. I was staying with an astrologer who looked at Laurie's chart instantly. She discovered that Neptune was badly aspected for Laurie that day. It was a day when drugs or poisons could dangerously interfere with Laurie's health.

We both prayed as we drove for three hours to get to Laurie. All the while I was doing my wheeling and dealing with God again, asking that her life be spared. When we arrived, the swelling of Laurie's tongue was half-way down and she was having a boisterous time playing in the brightly painted pediatric ward with her fellow patients. By the time my visit was over, her tongue was back to normal. The swelling was a puzzle. We never knew what caused this extreme physical reaction. She had eaten her usual diet and there were no bite marks on her. She was released that evening. I am convinced that Laurie had a destined healing date with someone in the hospital that day.

With my habit of making deals with God, my commitment to give my life to teaching was made more deeply once again. I certainly seem to have a wavering connection to that service. Thankfully, Laurie is with me to keep me on my path.

Peter Kempers, another Dutch psychic and healer, married one of my dear friends, Anita. Peter and I had not met. Anita mentioned my name over dinner one evening. She shared that she wanted to drop into my workshop which was a few miles away. Instantly Peter demanded they rush to meet me. He told her he had been receiving psychic messages about me and for me. Until that moment had no idea who Ruthann Pippenger was. After they entered the venue, Anita explained all of this to me in English. Peter did not speak English. I agreed to accept his help the following Sunday, on May 1. I presented my new teacher spiritual guide and his wife with a nosegay of lilies of the valley. Peter did the work for which it seemed my soul had contracted him to do. He continued to mentor me and guide me spiritually like an older, wiser brother. He often assured me that Laurie was a master and she meant to keep me on the path. He reminded me over and over that even though Laurie was a masterful soul, she really needed to be socialized. She needed to know that I was the boss of the family. He said it was a rare opportunity for me to learn to maintain equality with her soul. My work blossomed and grew under Peter's tutelage.

Within a short time, my students in Holland were encouraging me and helping me to create another organization called Peace Through Understanding to carry on my work. I had received the name of the work in meditation in the early 70s. Then Paul Solomon gave a psychic reading for me during the Forty Days in the Wilderness training. That reading in 1977 stated that my work should be called "Peace Through Understanding." I continued teaching ILC. And I definitely felt freer to begin developing The Living Together Skill tools and techniques into workshops. My career blossomed. As my dear friend Rina Vergano said: "Everyone needs The Living Together Skills!" And I was pleased to offer the skills in workshops more often.

In the Netherlands, it became apparent that stairs spaced other than the usual modern American scale terrified Laurie. If a staircase was in a three hundred year old walk-up in Amsterdam, Laurie was threatened. Old Dutch buildings through hundreds of years of construction probably did not have official building code specifications. Many old steps are narrow and most are very steep. Individual steps can even be different heights in the same stair case. In older homes, stairs normally curve toward the top to a landing to facilitate the transit of caskets. If Laurie encountered an open modern spiral staircase often used in newer Dutch buildings, she was resistant to use the steps and could become nearly unmanageable. Oftentimes, I found her fear sorrowful, pitiable, and at times irritating. At that time, I thought her terror was only because of depth perception difficulties.

One evening, we were eating at our favorite Greek restaurant in The Hague. It is in an elegant centuries old building that sits across from The Parliament Buildings' reflective pool and Swiss style fountain. We lived a few blocks away and enjoyed meeting dear friends there several times a year. Laurie adored the restaurant's ambiance and menu and would jump at the chance tonight to be there again if we could. One weekend evening, we arrived with a party of ten later than usual. The restaurant was packed. For the first time ever we were seated upstairs. We were taken up the modern front steps which were long, elegantly wide, evenly spaced with grand brass banisters. That was no problem for Laurie. Our secluded table was toward the rear of the restaurant.

When dinner was over, the server guided us down the back stairs, which were extremely narrow—maybe two feet wide, very steep, and with no railing. Laurie flipped out and cried hysterically. She was about nine at the time. Half way down the flight, she screamed out, "These steps could kill me! These steps will kill me!" Irritated and embarrassed, I hushed her and reassured her that they would not. I had to remind her that her dear

Here I Am!

friend, "Papa Nico" was in front holding her and I was behind holding her. We would protect her. She let out a loud "Whew!" when we reached the ground floor. Looking up at me with bulging eyes of fear, she declared, "Those steps could have killed me!"

I again did my motherly one-liner blah-blah-reassurance that her she was safe. And then I bolted, sensing to my core how deeply this phrase was programmed into her subconscious mind. It was charged with intensity. I understood it was a past life program and had nothing to do with this lifetime. I realized that she must have fallen to a death on stairs in a recent lifetime.

Zing! Zang! Zoom! As I remember those moments and the next minute, my body tingled with electric energy. My auric field felt expanded, translucent and fairy fine. My body was swaying in slight circles as the chakras expanded. And my mind raced through nine years of collected but disconnected vignettes. I swooned yet managed to stand as I remembered that Murshid Samuel Lewis died after being in a coma as the result of falling down stairs in 1970. The fact that Laurie had been called a master soul so many times flew through my mind. The fact that Paul stated that Laurie appeared to him as an old man with great powers and a strange sense of humor hit me. I recalled that Samuel Lewis was considered a master teacher in three traditions and was known for his eccentric humor.

I heard our friends buzzing about how delicious our meal had been and giving Laurie sweet attention, yet my mind raced in multiple layers of conscious, subconscious, and superconscious memories. In less than two or three minutes, it seemed that my soul was hurling numerous flaying puzzle pieces that stripped away my ignorance of her soul into a solid picture of her being-ness. The following memories zipped through my mind:

I remembered Sufi camp participants huddling and cooing over infant Laurie who slept through much of the day. Until this moment I had not I understood their fascination with Laurie. Was it Sam they sensed?

Pir Vilayat Inayat Khan blessing and naming Laurie, Rafaeli, after the archangel of healing. He assured me that she had great healing powers, should never live in a big city, would not be very disabled, and would be wonderful with small animals. Experienced campers seemed awed and told me that it was rare and auspicious to have an archangel's name bestowed by Pir Vilayat.

Laurie calling the Buddha statues in the Chicago Art Institute, "Gawd" with Sufi-like breathless reverence. I realized then that she had a Buddhist background in a recent life. Buddhism was one of the paths Murshid Sam followed. He was recognized as a Buddhist Zen Master, a Jewish scholar, and a Sufi Master.

The fact that she had the hottest little healing hands I had ever felt registered suddenly and fit together with stories of Murshid's mastery of healing and expertise at teaching healing. Laurie's father specialized in healing under the auspices of Murshid Sam. I had read years earlier that Murshid Sam sent bolts of healing energy where needed. I recalled Laurie playing "toss the energy" with Paul and other healers at The Fellowship.

Murshid started the Sufi Dancing movement (now The Dances of Universal Peace). I felt Laurie in the womb stepping in rhythm as if dancing and tapping as if drumming. Even the fact that she was attracted to and adored anybody that dressed or acted like a hippie went zinging through my mind. Sam was called the Guru of the Haight-Ashbury Hippies in the 60s.

My Name Is Laurie

I remembered an afternoon with two Dutch dance leaders in Holland. They shared extensively with me about the Dances of Universal Peace in Europe. As they drove us to the train station, they asked about my activities. I told them I was directing an organization called Peace Through Understanding. They said, "Oh. That is interesting! Did you know Murshid Sam had an organization called Peace Through the Arts?" Strangely, I felt an internal bolt and an intriguing shock. I calmly assured them I had not known that fact. Laurie had twisted around and stuck her head between the two front seats, and, with a mischievous smile, she looked me straight in the eyes and melodically exclaimed, "I *love* the arts!" Never in her life had she said anything like that. Normally, she did not respond to adult conversations. I was startled by her response yet prevented any connection from kicking in. That had been too early for this realization that was now bumping and buzzing, zinging and zapping, and flailing through my mind.

I remembered reading two little books I found in Weisser's lower Manhattan bookstore about Murshid Sam. One was *In the Garden,* and the other one was self published. I lost it, forgot the author's name and the title, and have never found any of Sam's students who remember the book or the statement that touched my heart. However, I clearly was struck when reading that book that Murshid Sam was so perturbed at being repeatedly called a "dirty old man" when he extended his love that he had stated, "When I come back, I am going to be a retarded little girl and give all the love I want." Thousands of incidents of Laurie bestowing love on streets, airplanes, buses, trams and in restaurants, schools, churches, at resorts and healing conferences flashed before me. People had accepted her love, hugs, and kisses without stipulation because she was "just" a cute Down syndrome girl, who (they believed) didn't know better.

In just moments, these memories all flashed through my mind. I continued in this altered state as I walked with my head in the clouds with my dinner companions from the old servant stairs in the rear to the front door of the restaurant. Still reeling, I heard myself thinking: *"Oh, my goodness, she is the reincarnation of Murshid Samuel Lewis!"* Finally, I understood who this masterful soul was expressing.

My dear friend, Djouni, noticed I was looking stunned and asked if I was okay. I said as effortlessly as possible, "Oh, I seem to be deep in meditation. I'll be okay in a few seconds. I need a few deep breaths of fresh air." It was too soon to share my realization, and I needed to digest my awareness.

As I journaled that evening, I wondered why Sam had chosen me to be his mother. It was easier to understand why he would choose Saul to be his sire. I could not help myself from speculating what a situation it would be if your spiritual teacher came back as your illegitimate special needs child and you refused to recognize him. From what I heard and read, that would definitely be a Murshid Sam style in-your-face-teaching! Was Sam testing Saul? I had heard Saul's real father left his mother and him at age two. I was curious about that karma. It is not really my business, yet I found it fascinating. Years later, I learned that Murshid Samuel Lewis and his father were not on the best of terms. Both of these men had "fathering" issues. Did this incarnation with such peculiar fathering issues help the two of them fit together like a hand and a glove?

I, of course, believe in reincarnation. I do understand that my belief that Laurie is the reincarnation of Murshid Samuel Lewis is more than most people (especially Ruhaniat Sufis) want to accept. Please also note that Sufi teachings do not recognize reincarnation as such. I think their wording would be "a soul makes an impression on a lifetime." Murshid Samuel Lewis, a Buddhist scholar, undoubtedly believed in reincarnation.

Here I Am!

Through the years I spent with The Fellowship of the Inner Light in the Netherlands and Norway, the steady part of my income came from facilitating past life regressions and helping people understand and resolve karmic lessons. The far memory of primal therapy training and the teachings of The Fellowship easily moved me into experiencing numerous past lives personally and doing regressions for others. Paul Solomon and Peter Kempers had both assured me that I had been a priestess in many lifetimes and had helped people learn to resolve their karma and to make positive choices by examining and forgiving past life memories. Incidentally, both of them had also told me that my life was meant to be a teaching to others. I often chuckle about my foolish errors and think, "Yes, my life is a teaching of what not to do!"

Occasionally, I ponder the fact that Murshid Samuel Lewis had an organization called Peace Through the Arts. I have wondered, "Did Laurie come to me to help further her Peace Through the Arts work by helping me with Peace Through Understanding?" She has done the latter over and over by inspiring participants and empowering them to be more self-expressive and unconditionally loving. She often expresses regret that so little has happened with Peace Through Understanding in the last eleven years in the United States.

I hope this excerpt on Murshid Sam from the Peace Works Publication Web site is beneficial in your understanding:

> *"The originator of the Dances of Universal Peace was Murshid Samuel Lewis. A life-long seeker, he studied and mastered many spiritual paths, and was the first American-born Sufi master. Committed to world peace through exchanges in the arts and agriculture, he was a 'citizen diplomat' long before the phrase was invented. 'Eat, Dance and Pray Together' was his peace plan. In his writings and teaching talks, he especially credits two of his teachers, Hazrat Inayat Khan and Ruth St. Denis, for their influence on him as the Dances began to 'come to and through' him."*

At most Peace Through Understanding gatherings we would "Eat, Dance and Pray Together." We used only two dances from The Dances of Universal Peace that I remembered from Sufi Camp. However, we began almost every gathering with spiritual dances that originated at Findhorn, a spiritual retreat center in Scotland.

I decided to keep this realization of Laurie as Murshid Sam to myself. I knew most people would think I was crazy. Then, later in 1987 while teaching a thirty-day summer retreat, participants were talking about Laurie's ability to create changes and magic in their lives. Each day they had been observing, sharing, or hearing about her power to teach various participants in a great variety of ways. As I was closing an afternoon teaching session, the group sincerely asked me for an explanation. "How does Laurie work her magic in our lives? How does she know what to do or what to say?"

I hesitated, closed my eyes, and silently questioned myself, is this the appropriate time and the appropriate audience to reveal my knowledge? My intuition assured me that this was the correct time and place. And then, I shared the evening with the flashes of realization and flushed out the history of her life and the commonality to Sam's life. The group silently and respectfully registered what I shared. I concluded: "And that's why I believe Laurie is the reincarnation of Murshid Samuel Lewis, the guru to the San Francisco Hippies."

Our rather grand retreat venue was a stately Belgium "hunting lodge." As I finished that sentence, immediately there was a child's knock for entrance at the teaching room door. Laurie peeped her head around one of the towering carved double wooden doors, swept the room with her eyes, smiled impishly, announced loudly and theatrically, "Here I am!" and, after a perfectly held pause, stepped backward and closed the blessed door. End of message! Everyone was stunned into silence. Then everyone roared with laughter at her impeccably timed confirmation!

And my dear friend and colleague, Jan Ton, shouted "Well, I'm a believer!"

8 Rafaeli at Work

*"I have found the paradox, that if you love until it hurts,
There can be no more hurt, only more love."*

~ Mother Theresa

There are literally thousands of people to whom Laurie has given her love in abundance. As a young child, she seemed to have no constraints in sharing her loving attention. On a single bus ride or tram ride in the Netherlands, she might lovingly touch five or six people and influence everyone on the entire vehicle with her smiles.

The most moving incident for me of Laurie sharing unconditional love with someone was on a tram in The Hague. It was an untypically warm summer's day. As we boarded the tram, Laurie spotted an elegant, strikingly beautiful woman about fifteen years my senior. They beamed at each other. Laurie left my side to sit with the woman in the rear of the tram. I saw that Laurie was welcome and allowed her to do her "work." They cuddled and held hands, and Laurie kissed the woman's cheek. She leaned into Laurie and had tears in her eyes. She seemed to be relishing the contact, so I decided not to interfere. I continued to read my magazine. When it was time for us to exit the tram, Laurie did not come when I called her. I saw she was deeply involved and exchanging compassion with this woman whom she seemed to adore. I went back to take Laurie by the hand. As I greeted this poised woman, I was shocked momentarily. The inside of her left forearm bore the coarse telltale tattooed numbers of a Nazi prison camp survivor. The woman saw me startle at my visual discovery. She gave what I interpreted as a tender-knowing look goodbye. I managed to bid this woman a warm, silent nod and smile.

As we walked off the tram, I was carried away with sorrow. I found myself dealing with "what ifs." This woman would have been a teenager at the start of the war. I could only surmise that a beautiful teenage girl in a Nazi concentration camp survived after being forced into a sexual slave relationship with an officer, or worse, with any number of officers and guards. I could not help but wonder if her tears were also for Laurie. Nazis gassed people with cognitive disabilities. Laurie could never have lived in Nazi occupied countries without being hidden, experimented on, or ultimately gassed. My heart broke open, pulsing with pain, and I fought back my tears there on the street. Once again, I felt thankful and honored to escort and to protect Laurie in her work of sharing loving wisdom, compassion and tender understanding.

My heart was also broken open or chipped at many times in the company of Laurie and her classmate Kerstin, who is also Down syndrome and probably mosaic. For three years of what might be called middle school in the United States, Laurie and Kerstin were the only two students in their class at the Oslo Rudolf Steiner Helsepedagogisk Skole (School). On weekends, Kerstin's house was filled with siblings and their friends, so playdates there did not create many opportunities for the girls to be alone. Kerstin came to our home for Saturday afternoon playdates that culminated in dinner several times a year. When I walked through the foyer and looked into the living room as they danced, they appeared to glow at and through each other. Their smiles seemed divinely contented and more. Really indescribable. I am clairsentient and feel energies intensely. When I entered the room with them, my chest felt like it would explode and splinter into the infinite and my fingertips felt like they could shoot beams of light for thousands of miles. Rather than dare to experience the pain in my chest from their expression of cosmic love, I would escape. I would run into the kitchen to putz around. I often wondered how their school teachers could hold up through the holiness and explosive loving energy that the two of them generated.

They seemed to amp their energy down as the three of us would sit for our pasta dinners. I could be warmed and filled by their smiles and tenderness but not overwhelmed with my every cell tingling and my heart under pressure. I was with the two of them many times in the company of other people at school programs, Christmas bazaars, New Year parties, Kerstin's large birthday party between Christmas and New Years. In these gatherings, I did not experience the energy between them as overwhelming, just typically Down-syndrome–like: lovely, sweet, tender and heart-warming.

My hunch now is that, when they were totally alone and felt sheltered from outside energies, such as teachers, other students, or public view, they felt free to release, experiment with, and step up their capacities as masterful beings of love. Without disruptive forces, together in our living room, they seemed to practice and expand their energy fields and their capacity to be love. The Pure Love produced between the two of them was palpable. They seemed to magnify their normal earthly unconditional love into the universal "ocean of love" often referred to in the east. My chest could just not encompass or tolerate the Divine Love they emanated in private.

In the days following their playdates, I experienced our home as a temple brimming with the Holy Spirit. It felt more blessed than usual by Laurie's presence. Writing this, I wish I had been brave enough to yield to the experience, to lie down on the sofa, to enter meditation while they were in their exalted ecstatic state of joy and love and to allow it to wash over and through me. Only during some rituals of communion and in the very near presence of the Dalai Lama, Dagpo Rinpoche, Mother Meera, and Amma, "the hugging saint," have I felt this same quality of vibrant Divine energy.

Laurie started to withhold her energy publicly after we moved to Norway when she was about to turn thirteen. Privately we found Norwegians to be warm, kind, affectionate, generous, humorous, noble, and nonjudgmental friends. However, the culture of contained coolness of reticent strangers on the street in Norway, the often frigid temperature, plus her entering puberty were undoubtedly several of the causations of the change in her extending less love to strangers on the street and on buses and trams.

Laurie was really pleased when she could get an unknown Norwegian to smile as a "friend" on the streets of Oslo in the winter. We cherished our nine years living in Norway. From May 17, their independence day, to September 21, we found life especially joyful and pleasant. The sun was high in the sky and the reticence of strangers abated a bit on the streets, shops, and cafes. Certainly from September 21 to May 17 every year, I found the streets of Oslo chilling from more than dropped temperatures. I amused myself to tolerate the lack of autumn/winter smiles and eye contact on the street by singing a little ditty to myself: "Norwegians all smile in the summer. They forget how to smile in the fall. They begin to remember in springtime and in winter they all look like …, Well," etc. I did not sing the word hell because of Laurie. I held the word well with a fermata. Walking together on the sidewalks, Laurie grumbled and growled at me in typical teenage fashion when I mumbled my survival song. This ditty reminded me that the shining smiles would return in the summer.

When Laurie was fifteen, we went to Sufi Camp in the Swiss Alps. Following is the serendipitous story of how God and our souls brought us back to the Sufi Order.

In the early summer of 1991, while living in Europe, a persistent vision of blue skies, soft green rolling mountains, a beautiful blue lake and palm trees appeared to me. The vision occurred every time I sat quietly whether in meditation or not. It almost haunted me. I described it to several well-traveled people, and they could not identify my description. I knew I was seeing a place of beauty in Europe and knew it was not the Mediterranean. Needing to know what I was seeing led me to a book at The American Book Store in The Hague entitled *Europe on $50 a Day*. When I broke open the book, it opened to Lugano, Switzerland. There was the exact description of my meditations: a beautiful blue lake, surrounded by soft green mountains and palm trees. Better than that, it elaborated that Lugano was "the best of Italy and the best of Switzerland." It sounded like a perfect place for Laurie and me to vacation. I made the arrangements for our trip.

We enjoyed the train trip to Lugano traveling overnight on a sleeper car from Amsterdam. We woke up in Berne in time for coffee and croissants that were offered for sale on the train platform. Then there was the breathtaking morning ride through the soaring Swiss Alps. The vistas were replete with goats on hills and cows wearing bells, steeples appearing around mountain curves and many homes and even some barns hung with flower boxes filled with red geraniums.

Each day in Lugano, we enjoyed our adventures. I played Peter to Laurie's then-favorite character, Heidi. We took goat cheese deli-lunches up into the hills. Lugano is a perfectly sized city for Laurie and me to walk. We visited the same quiet churches daily where we lit candles for loved ones and, of course, world peace. We strolled along the elegant lake, watching retired locals and children throwing stale bread to the swans. We drank tart Italian sparkling lemonade at lovely cafes and allotted calories and time for a daily sundae at the open air Mövenpick ice-cream restaurant, where we listened to the soft jazz trio that played in the afternoons. We enjoyed the lakefront's long narrow park and the breath taking paintings in the 17th-century Villa Favorita**,** the home of the prestigious Thyssen-Bornemisza Museum.

I kept thanking God for giving me the intuition to find such a gentle beautiful and exciting vacation spot. As we were cutting through the piazza late one afternoon, we passed a café table where, surprisingly, shaven-headed Richard Baker Roshi and the teaching successor for Pir Vilayat Khan, Atum (Thomas) O'Kane were getting settled with two friends. I had not seen Baker Roshi, an American teacher of Zen Buddhism, for two years. We had last met at a conference entitled Death and Dying in the Black Forest of Germany. I stopped at their table to say hello. I was delighted that Baker Roshi introduced me to Atum. I did not want to impose on this auspicious group, so Laurie and I moved on.

We said goodbye to Baker Roshi and Atum. But Laurie kept flirting long distance with Baker Roshi as we walked up a narrow cobble-stone passageway to our hotel to change for dinner. It was the first day she was wearing a pink eyelet Swiss cotton ruffled dress with a history. Strange as it sounds, I was guided by a voice to cross a street and enter an Australian dress shop years earlier. As soon as I saw the just-ironed and hung dress, I knew it was a magical dress I needed to purchase but was never to consider mine alone. This expensive dress went to every mystery school retreat I directed. Laurie had seen it worn by many women. The dress, which seemed over the years to have developed healing qualities, helped women to get in touch with their free child, their little princess, or their tender nature. Laurie had wanted to wear this "princess" dress for years. She was finally tall enough to wear the coveted dress without fear of her tripping. She looked and felt like a pretty young woman. Her flirting and her whirling and twirling continued as we were about to turn a corner and miss the lovely smiles and acceptance aimed at Laurie from these two spiritual teachers who by now were both craning their necks watching her dance. Laurie seemed enchanted with Baker Roshi. At first I was surprised by the attraction between Baker Roshi and Laurie. Then I recalled a past life memory that I had experienced and I understood why they were responding to each other with intensity.

After comments by Paul about past life Egyptian connections in healing with Laurie, I had memories of Laurie being a male surgeon and of me being "his" wife and assistant in the healing temples of ancient Egypt. I remembered that we were so proud of our only son passing a series of initiations and reaching enlightenment. When I first met Baker Roshi, I thought that I recognized him as the reincarnation of that son. We had met at three different spiritual-psychological European conferences during the previous six years. We seemed to keep bumping into each other at conferences, on a conference dance floor in Amsterdam, and now in Lugano.

Suddenly, I understood why spirit had led us to Lugano. I knew that we had to go back to their table for a deeper contact for Laurie. We walked back down into the piazza. They appreciated Laurie's theatrics and immediately asked us to join them for a Coke. Baker Roshi and Atum explained they were teaching at the summer Swiss Sufi Camp nearby. They had come into town for a brief break. "Come to camp. It's in a beautiful setting. You will enjoy it." It was a wonderful idea. I rearranged our schedule. I rented a car for later in the week and then off we went to join the last two and a half days of camp.

As we arrived, Atum was "coincidentally" standing in the upper part of the parking lot available to us as we walked to register. Standing there in the open, I confided with him my long absence from the Sufi Order. I told him I had felt there was not enough room in the order for both Saul and me. It seemed natural and easy to share with Atum about Laurie's conception at the Woodstock Sufi Camp of 1975. He was understanding and welcomed me back into the fold. I also shared that I was convinced Laurie was a reincarnation of Murshid Sam. He nodded as he heard me, and I was not surprised when he did not add commentary.

Laurie touched and admired the woven purple, green, and black Guatemalan vest Atum was wearing. He literally took it off his back and gave it to her. She beamed and has been wearing that vest ever since! It is showing signs of wear. Each autumn I pull it out of storage, and each summer I choose to hide it. Laurie would wear the heavy cotton vest in the intense heat of the Virginia sticky summers if it hung in her closet. She tells me often that it has his love in it. It certainly has her love in it, too.

I shared earlier how Paul had warned me to keep Laurie's heritage secret to protect Saul and his students. At this camp, Laurie gave her first dictate to me about sharing her history. During Atum's teaching sessions at the camp, Laurie wedged herself into the circle so she could sit directly on his right. However at the last session, she surprised me by sitting next to me. It turned out to be an open microphone session. Laurie sat on my right in the circle directly across from Atum. I was curious why she changed her modus operandi. Atum opened with the ground rules for the afternoon: the microphone would be sent around the circle. It would be a "talking stick." Whoever held the microphone had the floor. Everyone was invited to share what was on their heart.

When the microphone came to Laurie, she handed it to me and said, "Tell them about my father."

I whispered, "No, Laurie.

Into the mike she said, "Tell them about my father!"

I said firmly shaking my head no, "No, Laurie, I don't want to."

Into the microphone she determinedly and calmly ordered, "Tell them about my father!" I looked at Atum and he nodded.

I gulped and began. I told the whole story of the "My Cosmic C-Movie" to the eighty or so people gathered: her conception at the Woodstock Sufi Camp in 1975, the letter and the phone call to her father, his denial of knowing me. I shared that my attraction to "the healing teacher" ended the day after our infamous "sleepover." His being married was an unacceptable reality. And the next day, he seemed to pretend he did not know me after sharing so intimately. This certainly meant that even friendship was an unacceptable reality. I also shared that I returned to Sufi Camp the next year when Laurie was three months old in 1976. It was the first camp held at the Abode of the Message. Pir Vilayat Inayat Khan was the main teacher. I said that I wrote a letter to Pir Vilayat explaining my situation with the birth of Laurie and that I had become pregnant with a teacher's child at the last Sufi camp. I asked for a meeting for counseling and advice. Saul was not at this particular camp. I submitted the letter to Pir Vilayat's secretarial staff, all males as far as I could see. When I inquired toward the end of the camp why I had not been called yet for an appointment, I was told in embarrassed and half apologetic energies that my letter had been lost. Two young men did not ask me to rewrite the story and did not arrange a meeting.

In my naïveté, I decided that if God saw to it the letter was lost; it was as it should be. I passively believed that I should just let it be. I never wrote another letter to Pir Vilayat, and I avoided the U.S. Sufi Order since that time. I shared that this was my first Sufi contact since 1977 and about how I met Atum and Baker Roshi in Lugano and accepted their suggestion to attend camp.

As people heard about the denial of Laurie by her nameless Sufi teacher father, many people started crying. At least eight people actually started sobbing. Some of the sobbing folk went deeply into screaming and releasing primal emotions. I can only suppose they were releasing past pains about distant fathers and feeling abandoned. Their neighbors in the circle held them, comforted them and encouraged them to release their sorrow. More than half of the circle cried before the story was concluded. Boxes of tissues were scooted and slid across the floor from one side of the tented platform to the other. As a primal therapist, past life regression therapist, I was not fazed by the commotion. Atum, a Jungian Psychologist, was not doing therapy. He was allowing people to express their emotions. Laurie was not thrown by the racket of people primaling either. In retreat programs, she had witnessed and oftentimes assisted rebirthing-type groups in which half of 38 people would be writhing, crying and/or screaming. She stayed put beside me as I talked. I had not expected so many emotional reactions from telling Laurie's story! The observer in me thought the drama trauma in the circle actually seemed comical. The therapist in me was gratified and humbled to be a catalyst for the healing experience of so many. The mother in me was amazed at Laurie's brilliance of knowing the right time and place to let people know about her father even though I still kept Saul's name hidden to the public.

When I finished, a distinguished middle-aged Swiss man stood up and said, "The Sufi Order owes you an apology. On behalf of the Sufi Order, I offer you an apology for this teacher's behavior!" I cried and thanked him. I felt some of the stiffness and defensiveness in my spine melt with that unofficial apology. I do not know who he was. I should have asked. Now, I think he was a leader of the European Sufi office and a local teacher. Anyway, his warm words of caring for how Laurie and I were treated by Saul were heartfelt and comfort me to this day.

My Name Is Laurie

When I finished with the story and accepted the apology, Laurie was contented and so was Atum. Laurie hugged me and thanked me. She smiled her knowing smile. Atum hugged both of us. Many people in the group thanked me for sharing so openly. People hugged and kissed both Laurie and me. And Paul was right once again, "Don't ever restrict Laurie from her work. She knows what she is doing."

Within the last year, I have mulled over and pondered about that lost letter at the Sufi Camp at The Abode of the Message. I have wondered about my passivity when I was told my letter was lost. Briefly I had thought, I could write another one there on the spot. I was so trained and brain-washed to accept God's will, that I lost all touch with the wisdom that "God helps those who help themselves!" I did not say, "Please give me a sheet of paper. I will rewrite the letter immediately." I laugh now as I am writing this. My personal assertiveness teacher was only three months old at the time and had not begun her work.

I have considered another possibility than the letter had been lost. The letter had undoubtedly been pre-opened by a secretary. I wonder now if the secretaries had been alerted that a delusional woman might appear at camp with a false claim of paternity. They might have been convinced, just as the social worker was, that I was an unbalanced student who was infatuated and obviously confused (lied) about the pregnancy. Certainly, if that was the case, it is another extension of my obvious negative karmic lesson with Saul. I forgive myself for needing this lesson and forgive the secretaries if they accidentally "lost my letter" to save Saul's honor. You see, I have finally awakened enough to wonder how the stressed secretary knew that my particular letter was "lost." I would think that, if a letter is lost, one does not know about its existence generally. But if it happened to be opened and read and then lost and the author appeared before me, as a secretary interested in right action, I would say, "Oh, wonderful you appeared! I forgot your name. I did not know how to find you. Your story is important. Let me quickly arrange a meeting with Pir Vilayat before the camp ends."

That did not happen, and fifteen years had ensued. The heartfelt apology was gratefully received and cherished. My heart was lightened.

Laurie has affected people through dancing. People often break into tears or delighted laughter when observing her dance. She enjoys dancing to entertain people. She has always danced and has taken some dance classes with spiritual friends. She had modern dance tutoring in Norway with Anne Britt Kjelsrud. Anne Britt, a warm person, has been a major influence in Norwegian modern dance and dance culture for several decades. They enjoyed floating around a small gym in a community center. Later, we made friends with two charismatic affectionate Trinidadian dancers. Laurie took street funk, jazz dancing, and Latin dance classes at two different dance schools from Jeffrey Carter and David Byer. Besides being empowering dance teachers, Jeffrey and David added much appreciated Caribbean island fire and joy to our lives during icy Norwegian winters.

When Laurie graduated from high school with a degree in Special Education Textile Arts and Crafts, she was asked to perform a dance solo for the school's commencement ceremony. The ceremony was held during a school day. The school included three educational programs, one for the deaf, one for the cognitively impaired, and one in draftsmanship and labor skills.

Surprisingly, the graduation ceremony ended an hour early. Laurie danced earlier than scheduled. I arrived just as Laurie was taking her bow. The audience was giving her a standing ovation. I heard some sobbing. As I looked around, the teachers of all three schools who were gathered at the back of the auditorium had tears in their eyes as she had danced to Mariah Carey's song, "Hero." I have witnessed this effect over and over. She danced in a review for The Celebration Center Church in Falls Church, Virginia to "My Heart Will Go On" and received a standing ovation from a tearful crowd. The same has happened several times at The Fellowship of Inner Light Church in Virginia Beach. Laurie moves people and opens their hearts and minds to the possibilities of what can be done with less-than-perfect material.

Paul Solomon had told me when Laurie was an infant that she came into this lifetime to prove that you could do a lot with less-than-perfect material. He explained that she had taught that message as a doctor and a healer in many lifetimes and people did not get it. So, she decided she would come in with Down syndrome to personally prove to others that it could be done.

After one of these performances at the church with Laurie, a size eighteen, a fifty-year-old visitor who was a size two and a professional dancer came up to me. She spoke eloquently about Laurie's ability to move energy and people's hearts. I find it hard to put this in writing—she actually said that Laurie was the best dancer she had ever seen. She said that Laurie moved energy better than anyone she had ever witnessed. She confessed that, "Because of my profession, I have been obsessed with beauty and youth. I am having plastic surgery tomorrow so I can continue to look young. I feel I must do this to maintain my career. Laurie's dancing made me realize anyone of any shape or condition can dance and move an audience with love. I wish I could trust that about myself without surgery."

A few months later, I saw a performance by Marcel Marceau, the great mime. Watching him from the balcony of the Ford Theater, I realized that he was doing more than telling stories in mime. He was moving masses of energy in his performance. His movements—and not the mime stories—reminded me of Laurie's dance moves. I suddenly understood the professional dancer's assessment of Laurie. It dawned on me that watching Laurie dance is like watching a Tai Chi master move energy. Her movement of energy with charisma, attention, and purpose is what touches an audience.

From ages nine to eighteen, Laurie insisted that, at every party/gathering she attended, she should be allowed to sing songs to the audience. At that time, she could not carry a tune. So her songs seemed more like out-of-tune chants. Her words were specifically channeled for each person and her movements and face were heartwarming to witness. Musically, her songs were excruciating to hear. With great poise, she would stand before the group. She dramatically gestured with her healing hands toward individuals and sang simple loving lyrics to them.

She would spend two or three minutes singing to each person, often repeating herself. The words she extended with deep eye contact, total devotion, unconditional acceptance and respect typically were "You are so wonderful," "You are so beautiful," "I love you," "I love knowing you," "God loves you," "You are so cute," "You are so handsome," "Give your love," "You are so nice; you are so kind," "You are love," "You are my friend," "Remember God," "I love you so much," "You are such a beautiful friend," "I feel your love," et cetera. She was a howling Valentine.

After each person's "verse," she bowed her head in deference to them. Half of the audience would be in tears and the other half would be wincing and cringing from the dreadful sounds that had emanated from her adoring face and smiling lips. I winced while watching others in the audience cringe and roll their eyes. She could spontaneously go on for many minutes and her captive audience would become restless. I normally stopped her before she felt finished. I felt embarrassed and proud of her at the same time. There were times when I wondered if she was testing her audience to see if they could receive loving adoration through such horrific sounds.

I am unaware when, how, or why this tradition stopped. I often miss this portion of Laurie's "work." Interestingly enough, she now sings on key at least half of the time. I wonder if she is too self-conscious to extend this technique of love to others because of her age.

Stories of Laurie's influence and impression on others still continue to come to me. Remember Brie Jontry, the three year old who knew Laurie's name before I believed I was pregnant? This story came to me from Brie. She is now the mother of Noor. Brie stated that it seemed impossible, but Noor said that she remembered Laurie from her infancy.

> *"When I told Noor we'd be seeing you and Laurie, but doubted she'd remember you both as she was only a few weeks old when you last visited, Noor said,*
>
> *'I remember the girl held me and if felt like I was in the ocean.'*
>
> *Oh, I said, she held you in the rocking chair.*
>
> *'No, it wasn't the chair that rocked, it was her body. Like the ocean.'"*

Both Brie and I remembered that, when Laurie and Noor met, they had gazed at each other for the longest time. The infant and the twenty-eight year old looked enchanted and as if they were in a world of their own. I am reminded that the Hindus and Buddhist often talk of the "ocean of love" being felt in meditation or emanating from masterful beings. I suspect that what Noor felt and remembers is Laurie sharing that "ocean of love" with her.

There has been a new development in our life together in the past few months. Laurie now regularly says to me, "Feel the Spirit of Love," "Be the Spirit of Love," or "Feel the Holy Spirit." I realize that she is attempting to train me to handle all situations with the spirit of Divine Love. She admonishes me to release all irritations or small hiccups in life even as insignificant as two papers sticking together. I am delighted with my personal guide who reminds me several times a day to step into the essence of stillness and compassion. It's not working totally yet, and Laurie is persistent.

Lest I forget who Laurie is and my responsibility to her compassionate work, the Universe sent me two reminders on November 1, 2008 that primed me to write her story. A few minutes before Samuella Alston asked me when I would write the book about Laurie, Mary Elizabeth Marlow stopped for a quick chat before I spoke at The Fellowship's Sunday service. Mary Elizabeth and I met when I was pregnant with Laurie. We had both been teaching and coaching the skills of ILC since that time. This day she came to reveal that her dear colleague and co-author, Joseph Rael, a Native American Shaman, had shared with her that Laurie was a "Master Soul". I thanked her sincerely for delivering this message.

I shared with her that our dear friend, Gerd Bjørke, had ten years earlier given me the same message. Joseph, also known as Beautiful Painted Arrow, had assured her that Laurie was a "Master Soul". Laurie and I had joyfully met Joseph at Gerd's home in Oslo on several occasions for private healing sessions. After one of these appointments, he had lightheartedly commented to her that Laurie's healing energy and personality were so strong that he imagined that many people found her (and me for that matter) overwhelming. He admired the fact that Gerd, Laurie and I came together as extended family with our common interest in cultivating the spirit of peace.

9 The Linguist, the Foodie, and the Model

"… often the mere sharing of recipes with strangers turns them into good friends."

~ Jasmine Heiler

For many years Laurie did not speak clearly. It was heartbreaking to Laurie that she could not make herself understood. Often Laurie's listeners were embarrassed that they could not interpret what she was attempting to say. Her little face would drop when she was not understood. I felt sorry for both of us when it was necessary to say two or three or even more times, "Honey, please try again, I don't understand." Teachers and I thought it was only a normal Down syndrome speech impediment caused by the shape of the mouth and generally larger tongue. We did not realize that her hearing was seriously impaired and caused a great deal of the mispronunciation.

Unfortunately, Laurie had several ear infections as a baby and toddler, which undoubtedly caused her hearing loss. It is fortunate for us that her strongest hearing level is at my voice range. She does not hear high-pitched sounds or low-pitched sounds well including the smoke detector unless she is under it. High female voices used to drive her to maddening distraction, especially if there were three or more women laughing. She actually woke up several times when I was entertaining because of this. She would run into the living room, holding her ears, looking tortured, most often crying, and then demand, "Stop! Stop laughing, you hurt my ears!" The range of most adult male voices is difficult for her to hear. Men must always speak louder to be heard, even when she is wearing hearing aids.

When Laurie was an infant, I constantly had to remind myself that I needed to speak to her so that she could learn language. We are both quite psychic and relish silence. I saw it as a daily duty for me to speak often enough to her to stimulate her language skills. It was a great delight one day in the car when I realized that her finger pointing and her "Ah dah?" actually meant "What's that?" Since then, I have heard one preverbal "normal" baby use "Ah dah" in the same way. I have pondered—do all babies start early with the same "Ah dah"?

I had been responding to her "Ah dah's" with appropriate information. It was a relief to know she was actively involved in our communication. When she was two years old, she was insatiable for several weeks about wanting to learn the names of everything in sight. At that time, words went into her brain and almost never came out of her mouth.

When she was sixteen months old, we stayed temporarily in a cottage in Virginia Beach near a pond where a family of ducks was in residence. Each evening after dinner I would walk her or carry her to see the ducks. One night in my arms, with perfect enunciation, she looked at me and said, "Go see the ducks!" It was her first sentence, perfectly pronounced. I was taken aback, delighted, and encouraged!

When she was three, she stood to the right of my table setting after every meal, graciously smiling with adoration in her eyes and strength in her stance. Laurie obviously wanted to serve me with an invisible object. She would say, "Yucky gucky?" I was embarrassed for being so unaware and out of touch to not comprehend for many weeks that my little waitress's "Yucky gucky?" meant, "Do you want a cup of coffee?" When I came to my senses, I thought what I have said so many times throughout the years, "Dear God, who is the one with the cognitive impairment here?"

Laurie learned to speak both Dutch and Norwegian quite well. Neither The Fellowship of Inner Light nor Peace Through Understanding had funding to pay for American or English schools when we lived abroad. Laurie attended local schools and was therefore forced into an educational setting in which she had to learn the languages. I always worked in English and have little patience or skill for learning languages. So she learned to speak both languages better than I did. I learned enough to keep up with her and the green grocers. Again I asked the question, "Dear God, who is the one with the cognitive impairment here?"

Dutch is a language that is perfect for the shape of the Down syndrome mouth and larger-than-normal tongue. Much of the Dutch language is either quite forward in the mouth or quite guttural in the back of the mouth and therefore easy for a larger tongue. Laurie preferred to speak Dutch over English. I empathized with her reasoning: people understood her Dutch better than her English.

On one of my trips abroad, I hired a temporary nanny to stay with Laurie in The Hague. The woman was English and had been a long time resident of the Netherlands. She spoke Dutch fluently. I left her with the admonition that only English was to be spoken in our home. I warned her that Laurie would try to speak Dutch with her. I explained that I felt deeply within my core that we would return to the States to live someday; therefore, Laurie's English needed to be consistently maintained in our home.

After a week, the nanny called me and regretfully exclaimed, "Laurie has forgotten *all* of her English. I have to speak Dutch with her."

I exclaimed back, "I'm sorry, *you* have been outsmarted! Believe me; Laurie is not so dumb that she forgot her English in one week. She is smart enough to make you *think* she forgot her English! Please tell her that Mama told her she speaks Dutch at school and English at home—period!" We both giggled, and Laurie lost that language skirmish.

There is a deep longing in Laurie to have perfect hearing. Oftentimes I think she detests her hearing loss more than the diagnosis of Down syndrome. The hearing loss makes her declare that she is "not normal," and she considers herself normal otherwise. During the Clinton administration, to ease her embarrassment and shame of her hearing loss, I reminded her that President Clinton wore hearing aids.

When she was younger, I observed over and over that she had a real resistance to listening to others, especially to me. This I saw as a karmic soul lesson that might account for the need to deal with a hearing loss. Up to two years ago, she would actually turn off her hearing aids in front of someone to make the point: *I am not willing to listen to you.* She has since developed a willingness to listen to friends, case managers, supervisors, and me. Obviously, that has made our life together easier.

Her first hearing aid, a bulky over-the-ear model that she despised, was prescribed in Norway. Before wearing the hearing aid, she seemed to mimic Norwegian lilts like a Minnesota comic. It was comical yet sad. She could obviously not sort out the high lilting intonations of the language. With the hearing aid, her Norwegian language skills improved dramatically. Laurie now has two nearly invisible hearing aids that benefit her. Generally, she is not embarrassed to wear them. Her vocabulary continues to expand, and her speech is clearer than ever before. Sometimes she seems to surprise herself when she uses a five-syllable word correctly. My delight is obvious to her, and our conversations have become more interesting. Friends who only see her in intervals of a year always remark with amazement about her language improvement.

Laurie is definitely a foodie. Sharing and learning about food together is an important part of our family life. From the beginning, she enjoyed the kitchen setting. She sat on the kitchen counter in an infant seat from the time when she was a few days old. She has been taught to prepare food since she could stand on a stool and reach the kitchen counter. Preparing meals together is one of the joys of our life together; serving and preparing food is a large part of Laurie's life. From the time Laurie was walking until about age nine, she was fascinated with restaurant kitchens and attempted to enter them. She has always been welcome in the kitchen and enjoys helping prepare the table and food. Sometimes I am not welcome in the kitchen as she cooks. She feels appreciated and happy when making meals beautiful and enjoyable.

Sadly, when her young cognitively impaired friends visited, they shared that they were never allowed in their kitchens. They tentatively accepted our invitations into the kitchen to help prepare meals. They cautiously learned to wash vegetables and tear salad greens. They beamed with pride at making their first vegetable or fruit salad. Laurie relished playing the teacher and master chef. All of this was before she watched cooking shows on television.

Currently, all educational programs that I know of offer food preparation as a life skill to people with cognitive disabilities in high school and later learning programs. Laurie adored her cooking classes in school. She proudly shelves her class recipe notebooks with her recipe books. She enjoys sharing recipes. Laurie often talks about food and recipes at the checkout counters of grocery stores with her "new friends." She asks the person behind her what they will be making with their purchases and shares what she will be doing with hers.

Very early on, Laurie's creative abilities and love of beauty were obvious in meal presentations. She made salads independently at age four. By twelve she was making a killer dressing, identified by some as the best that they have ever tasted and that it should be marketed. Recently someone asked, "Didn't she learn it from you?"

And I responded, "Yes, she learned the basic vinaigrette from me. However she is creative and much more daring than I am. She changes it a bit each time and almost always it is fabulous."

When Laurie was three and four, we stopped occasionally at the Southern Kitchen restaurant in New Market, Virginia. Laurie always pre-empted the hostess and took over her position. Graciously, with a big smile and a grandiose, sweeping gesture of welcome at the door, Laurie handed out menus and led people to empty booths. Laurie beamed with importance. Everyone was charmed by the mini-hostess.

When Laurie was twenty-eight years old, we stopped at the Southern Kitchen late one evening for a break and a snack as we headed back to Washington, DC. An older female customer came up to us and inquired, "Is this the girl who used to help me give out menus and seat people many years ago?" The cashier, the same one from years ago, the retired hostess, and Laurie all laughed together at the stories. The retired hostess shared that she often wondered where and how Laurie was. It was a warm and appreciated, unscheduled reunion with many hugs and kisses. How fortunate Laurie had been to be allowed such freedom of expression and caring at a young age.

From the time Laurie was three through eight, I was filled with trepidation every time we entered a new restaurant in the United States. As soon as we ordered, Laurie determinedly headed for the kitchen with wonder in her eyes. In each new restaurant, I would gulp and wonder how her eagerness would be received. It surprised me that she almost always was allowed to peek in for a minute. Whenever she could get away with it, she would also play hostess until her food arrived at the table. I was often embarrassed when I had to deal intimately with the restaurant manager or staff. However, I remembered Paul's message to let Laurie do her holy work.

As I share this, I now realize the importance of restaurants to Laurie. They were actually temples of service to her. It was her favorite place to captivate strangers. She instantly created an atmosphere in which patrons were given an opportunity to open their minds and hearts to unconditional love. This undersized lover's magnetism was almost always welcomed. I am sure that people sometimes muttered internally, "Well, she doesn't know any better. After all, she's cognitively impaired." Out loud they would say the "She's so cute" mantra to me with a smile.

When we moved to Europe, Dutch restaurant staffs were less likely to show her the kitchen, and she was never allowed to hand out menus. Laurie does not let much deter her. So she creatively adjusted her modus operandi. Laurie then carried out her mission by walking from table to table as a diminutive maître d' and cordially asking the diners if everything was okay. She would touch their shoulder or arm, cock her head, smile, and simply say, "'kay?" Then she would linger a few moments to get the smiling reports. Almost everyone was intrigued by her devoted attention during table visits. Often her intrusions ended with cuddles and squeezes. As she left she would say, "Eet smakalijk," the Dutch equivalent of bon appétit.

I can never forget the Sunday night when we stopped for a bite at a neighborhood snack shop minutes before it was to close. The only other customer was an aged man sitting at the counter who literally had about five white hairs left on his head. I imagine he was over ninety-five years of age. I sensed, correctly or incorrectly, that he was very lonely. As I was paying at the counter, Laurie went up to him, hugged him, gently pulled him toward her, and kissed him on the cheek. I remember that he actually bent his head to her for a lingering moment. He seemed to absorb her energy and attention, although he never looked at her. Before moving away, she patted his arm as if to say, "You are important to me and I bless you." The counterman nodded his head to me and ever so slightly grinned approval.

In this instance and others, as an observer of Laurie's caring, my heart felt like it was exploding with love. Laurie distributed love for both of us. I wondered then and still wonder, when will I ever be willing to do this work independently? Sometimes I give this quality of love to friends and students, and I do send loving thoughts each day to strangers. However, I want to dare to be like Laurie and give unconditional love to strangers in this body as Ruthann. Certainly, as an adult, Laurie is more cautious and constrained in sharing physical touches with strangers.

Laurie cherishes her accumulation of cookbooks. I give her one for almost every birthday and for Christmas. This was the only reading Laurie would do with me after graduating from high school. So for several years, we spent every Sunday afternoon reading recipes.

The Linguist, the Foodie, and the Model

Fortunately, for several years, Laurie has cooked dinner for the two us with some guidelines on oven temperatures and timing from me. Two nights are completely ritualized, and I am usually ordered out of the kitchen. Friday is her low-fat pizza night, and Saturday is rice pasta. Weekly, she alternates sauces. I look forward to our two weekly food routines: watching PBS cooking shows on Saturday afternoons and cooking together on Sunday evenings. We also enjoy planning holiday meals and small dinner parties together.

It was fortuitous that I took personal time from work one morning for Laurie to meet Julia Child at a book signing. It was two months before Julia passed away. It is definitely one of the highlights of Laurie's life. She was amazingly patient as we sat on the sidewalk in a long line for two hours before the store opened. Then as we stood in line for an hour and a half snaking through the store aisles. She did not complain. She did comment, "This is taking a long time!" I agreed.

I was mildly startled and surprised when Julia's assistant nudged Julia's elbow and pointed Laurie out while we were back six places in line. Julia smiled pleasantly at Laurie. Laurie excitedly smiled back. Julia smiled more widely. Laurie out-smiled her. Julia's smile got bigger, and so did Laurie's. It appeared to be a private smiling contest! They were both beaming when Laurie was actually handed the book! Laurie has an amazing memory and values that book and those precious moments with her idol.

Currently, her favorite TV cook is Lidia Bastianich. She has longed for years to meet Lidia. Every Sunday, Laurie memorizes the TV Guide's cooking show schedule so that she does not miss her on the coming Saturday. A rare opportunity took place during the rewrites of this book. For a 2009 Christmas present, I took Laurie to Lidia's talk at the Smithsonian Resident Associate Program entitled, "Cooking and Life in the Heart of Italy." Lidia was warm, charming, and humorous. I realized later that her cooking shows are a serious business and are packed with information. She does not have the time to be as relaxed as she was in a discussion format. There was a book signing afterward. I bought Lidia's newest book to be Laurie's Christmas recipe book.

As we reached Lidia, she respectfully asked Laurie if she could hug her. Laurie, of course, agreed. Standing and facing each other at the end of the signing table, Lidia and Laurie shared several minutes of tender hugs and discussion about Laurie's cooking. I was moved by Lidia's acceptance of Laurie. Lidia said sweetly to her, "I'm glad you enjoy cooking. You are so nice and so pretty." Laurie seemed to enter a surreal space.

As we walked away through the long corridor, Laurie said, "You are like Lidia, Mom."

I said, "Thank you. She is wonderful. That is a wonderful compliment. But what do you mean, I am like her?"

"Mom, you are both good mothers, loving mothers," My chest flooded with warmth as she squeezed my arm.

As we drove back home over the Potomac River, Laurie broke into an exalted mood. This experience with Lidia was a Merry Christmas moment for both of us.

Laurie dreams of having her own cooking show. My meager hope is to get some assistance so that she can share her low-fat pizza recipe and possibly other recipes on You Tube.

Laurie had two modeling opportunities in Oslo, Norway. She would love to do more modeling or even acting!

Laurie worked for Every Body Modell Castingagentur (Every Body Model Casting Agency). They specialize in providing interesting-looking people to the Norwegian advertising community. They also manage beautiful people. Every Body's office used to be one floor up from my office at Aurora, a healing center in downtown Oslo. After watching unusual characters dart ahead of me or climb the stairs with me, I went up one day and asked if they might be interested in having Laurie model. She came in to open a file, and a few photos were taken. The owner fell in love with Laurie's smile, dramatic charisma, and long chestnut red (dyed) hair. Several months later they called us. The first gig was to model winter fashions for the Oslo café rag, *Natt og Dag* (Night and Day). The photo shoot was an exciting evening with all the accoutrements: photographer, photographer's assistant, hair designer, makeup artist, stylist, music, lights, and fans. Laurie was in her element and danced for the photographer, who was delighted.

The hair designer enjoyed working with Laurie's waist-long, thick, chestnut red hair also. He spent an hour making a lacy tiara out of the front third of her hair. We were both enthralled and hoped to get copies of those photos. The photographs with that hair style were not published. Unfortunately the photographer did not keep or give copies to Every Body for Laurie's file.

Four years later, after moving back to the states, Every Body called Aurora and asked for our telephone number. Calling me in Arlington, Virginia, they thought that we were on vacation and asked Laurie to model in Oslo in five days. By an act of grace, I was home from work. I refused the offer and then called back twenty minutes later to ask about the modeling fee. As I hoped, her modeling fee would pay for her ticket. I nailed down two tickets for the price of one on that afternoon, and we were in Oslo in time for the shoot. It was a very welcome five-day trip back to our loving, extended family.

This time, the gig was for the association of practical nurses in Norway. Laurie was shown in magazine advertisements and on billboards with a handsome male practical nurse supposedly visiting her and drinking tea with her in her home. Roughly translated, the advertising slogans were:

"Sharing together is better than intravenous feeding."

"Caring is the medicine of the future."

Laurie certainly lives by those tenets!

10 Laurie Longs to Know Her Father

"Since everything is but an apparition, perfect in being what it is, having nothing to do with good or bad, acceptance or rejection, you might as well burst out laughing."

~ Long Champa

It seems that Laurie's soul moved Saul and me like great marionettes that evening on the cliff and bridge at the Sufi Camp in Woodstock, New York, to get the DNA she wanted. I certainly believe from Fellowship teachings and the quote below by Pir Vilayat Inayat Khan that Laurie definitely engineered her body and diagnosis. She obviously wanted to be "molded out of the fabric of her chosen parents and ancestors."

> *"Perhaps you decided to come to earth because you wanted to experience its unique environment. Or maybe your motivation was to make a mark, or to improve humankind's circumstances. ... to achieve these tasks, however, it was necessary to assume a body molded out of the fabric of your parents and ancestors; you chose them for the purposes of incarnation."* by Pir Vilayat Inayat Khan in Awakening: A Sufi Experience, Part 1.

During the first year of Laurie's life, only Paul Solomon, a few close friends, and I acknowledged her origins. In 1977, Paul suggested that I not reveal Saul's name to anyone, because it might threaten his relationship with his students. Paul inferred that announcing Saul as Laurie's father would result in bad karma for me. I acquiesced, wanting to be a "good and holy" spiritual student. So if people asked about Laurie's father, I said he was a Sufi leader and clarified that it was not Pir Vilayat Inayat Khan. I did not want to taint an innocent man's relationship to his students. I now believe that Paul's guidance to me was relevant for that time of "old-school thinking" and a male-dominated spiritual world. In fact, I now think he continued my childhood brain-washing to be a "good little girl." Of course, I had not been such a "good little girl" to get pregnant in a one-night stand with a married man. Paul strongly guided me to never reveal this important man's irresponsible actions. And for years, I did not.

As a trained family therapist, I believed in truth and transparency. Withholding the truth seemed self destructive to me. My family therapy mentor, Virginia Satir, taught: "Secrets drive people crazy." I was a firm believer of that axiom, and I still am. However, not knowing the karmic repercussions and trusting Paul as my spiritual guide, I did not reveal the name for years and was driven more than a little bit crazy by the stress of keeping Laurie's heritage to myself. In fact, writing this chapter has driven me a little bit crazy. As mentioned earlier, I have been dealing with the questions of what is relevant to reveal and just what is the reader's business and what is morally right. Only since 2003 have I revealed Saul's name in the relevant Sufi community, where I think it is appropriate for the truth to be known. Until then, I kept my secret carefully.

I believe everything is divinely planned and perfect. However, that does not always make every challenge or lesson easy to accept. I am well aware that I am human and live on a planet of duality that deals with right and wrong, yin and yang, up and down, morality and immorality, duty and irresponsibility. I am trained enough in cosmology to accept the theory that "we are all one." In the cosmic scheme of life, I understand that this story is a miniscule dot and an apparition. Because Laurie has requested me to tell about her father and because Paul Solomon and Peter Kempers both told me that I chose my life to be a teaching, I choose to share this aspect of Laurie's story with you.

This chapter and the next have been extremely difficult to write. Part of me thinks that the content of the chapters is nobody's business. I have eaten the material, burped it, and tried to digest it and assimilate it. I have spewed it out and am basically sick of it. Many times I have wanted to exclude it; yet I also received advice from my straightforward writing teacher to be honest and tell the complete story. I finally relaxed with this material when Venerable Dagpo Rinpoche, who is proclaimed to be the reincarnation of Marpa, The Translator (purportedly the best spiritual teacher that ever lived), advised me to tell Laurie's entire story. This one section of my life has been a melodrama. "My Cosmic C-Movie" continued.

In 1979 while keeping my secret of Laurie's father's name, I lived and worked alongside a European couple in the spiritual community, Carmel in the Valley. They shared with me that they met a Sufi teacher in Charlottesville and would bring him to Germany for a class. Yes—when they shared his name, this teacher was Laurie's sire. They had no idea that the giggling toddler they bounced in their arms was his child. When they enjoyed Laurie and her interest in their gourmet vegetarian food and music, it was very difficult to keep my mouth closed. I wanted to blurt out, "Oh, for goodness sakes, Laurie is Saul's child!" They probably would not have believed me. And he certainly would have denied it. This was within six months of Saul telling a social worker that he did not know me.

In retrospect, I know it is unfortunate that I also avoided talking to Laurie about her father. About twice a year in private I would say to her, "Your Papa's name is Saul and he is a great healer." When I was an "unwed mother" and pregnant with Laurie, people often said to me, "God is her father." I found that phrase comforting. Later I would tell Laurie, "God is your father." I realize now, that phrase made no sense to her. Laurie wanted a father who would actually throw her up into the air and catch her with giggles galore and who would read bedtime stories to her, rock her to sleep, hug and kiss her, and buy her ice cream cones.

And then one day in the Netherlands, Laurie burst wide open. She was ten years old. Completely distraught, she hysterically screamed at me with a flushed face and clenched fists from the long cold dark hallway leading to our kitchen, "You killed my father. You killed my father! I hate you. I hate you. You killed my father!"

Shocked, I ran to her. I knelt and assured her that I had not killed her father. At that moment she hated me so much, she would not let me hold her. As calmly and gently as I could, I asked her why she thought that I had killed her father.

She sobbed, "All children have fathers and mothers! I don't have a father! You killed him!" Laurie was attending a Dutch Catholic elementary school. All the children that she knew lived with fathers and mothers. There were no divorces in these Catholic families. Murder was the only option she could think of as to why she did not have a father. Her reasoning then was that I must have killed him. We had recently obtained a television with a cable connection. So possibly this style of thinking was triggered because she had watched just one too many American movies.

I felt panicked about her emotional state. I felt guilty that I had been depriving her knowledge of Saul. I calmed her down and assured her over and over, "I did not kill your father. Honey, I did not kill your father. I could never do anything like that." She relaxed some and allowed me to touch her. Cradling Laurie, I told her Saul's full name, where he lived. I continued to tell her the little I knew about him. We went into the living room. I wrote his name down for her. I taught her to read and to pronounce Saul's name. The name Barodofsky is a mouthful for a Down syndrome child. She announced that she wanted to see him and to be with him. I told her I understood. She wanted to add his last name to hers. That was not done and could not be done without his approval. In the privacy of our home, she called herself Laurie Shanti Pippenger Barodofsky.

That day, I promised her I would do everything I could to get her in relationship with her father. I prayed that the right opportunity would avail itself to us. On a trip back to the United States, I found a Pennsylvania Dutch-style family tree form. I filled it out for her with Saul's name and mine and framed it and hung it in her room. I filled in the missing data in her baby book. She was very proud.

In the meantime, we moved to Norway. The children Laurie was raised with at Carmel in the Valley were scheduled to be confirmed during a traditional ritual of adulthood at age fourteen, the summer of 1990. I decided that Laurie should join them. We participated in this ritual and blessing. It happened during The Fellowship Summer Gathering in Virginia Beach, Virginia. While in Virginia Beach, I felt almost obsessed to arrange a meeting with Saul. I wanted to know what he had become and if he finally would be willing to hear about Laurie's need for a relationship. I used an alias to get an appointment, in case he remembered my name from the letter before her birth, from the phone call after her birth, and from the visit from the social worker when she was a toddler. I was concerned that he would refuse access to me on the basis of my name. Little did I know what a deficient memory, by design or by denial, he appears to possess.

I felt strongly that I needed an opportunity to talk with him. This was before the internet existed. When I called for directions, I was guided to meet him in their home rather than his store. I was pleased, because this would provide more privacy for our meeting. During this call, his wife shared that she had sent him home from the store because he had chest pains and shortness of breath. It was years later that I discovered his wife is a nurse. Needless to say, when I heard he was experiencing troubling symptoms, I knew it would be terribly irresponsible to add more stress to his day by introducing myself as the mother of his child. The idea of his plopping over in front of me with a heart attack did not fit my mission!

When we greeted, it was obvious that he did not recognize me and did not know me by any name. I would not have recognized him on the street either. He appeared tired and haggard and his complexion was a dingy grey. I was amazed that he did not cancel the meeting with me. To me it is intriguing that his body responded so strongly on the day that I approached with positive prayer and wishes of harmony for all three of our souls.

He invited me into his kitchen, where he was preparing food. A brilliant red male cardinal was perched outside his kitchen window. Cardinals are my favorite bird species, and I missed them terribly in Europe. It was the first one that I had spotted on this trip, and he was spectacular. I took his appearance as an auspicious assurance that I had made the right decision to meet with Saul. Saul graciously shared a delicious cassoulet that he had prepared. He explained that Murshid Sam, his teacher, often greeted people with food. It was an ancient hospitable caravan tradition that Saul liked to maintain. So, as a traveler, I was welcomed with a delicious repast. It established a rapport.

My Name Is Laurie

I came to Saul with real questions about my relationship to The Fellowship of the Inner Light. We had a meaningful spiritual consultation. He was very helpful about several issues I had. He was down to earth, totally receptive, respectful, and he sincerely wanted to be of assistance. In addition to answering my question, he felt moved to share powerful stories of experiences he had with a woman named Mother Mary, whom he had visited on Mount Shasta. When he talked about Mother Mary Mae Maier, I felt a wave of holiness, calm, and blessing fall over the room.

I never mentioned having a child. He did not ask about partners or children. I asked if I could take a photograph of him. He agreed. Little did he know that the photograph was going on the parents' page of his child's baby book. As soon as it was developed, it went next to the photograph of me when I was eight months pregnant. Laurie was delighted to have a picture of her absent father and to have pictures of both of her parents. This was years before most people had Web sites. Now, she has any number of choices to find photographs of him.

We meditated in quiet for the second time in our student-teacher relationship of this lifetime. The meeting felt divinely guided; as mentioned earlier, it did not feel appropriate to announce to him on a day when he was experiencing heart symptoms, "Oh, by the way: I am the mother of your child, a Down syndrome daughter. Remember I wrote you a letter when I was pregnant? Remember I called you after her birth? Remember I sent a social worker to ask for a blood test?"

I left, confused and wondering how I should proceed. My hidden agenda remained locked away. I left, maintaining a hope that some break would come for Laurie to get her wish to know her father.

Three years later, when Laurie was seventeen, a stateside friend who lived in Saul's community called me in Norway. She revealed that there were new tough Virginia rulings on wayward fathers. DNA tests could now confirm paternity. Women were being encouraged to come forward. She advised me to come back and work with Charlottesville's Family Court before Laurie turned eighteen. After that time, it would not be possible to get legal support from the state.

Laurie and I came over in late summer 1993. I really wanted to avoid the court procedure. Naively, I hoped Saul would be receptive and agree to take the DNA test privately. I hoped for Laurie's sake that, once paternity was established, he would agree to have a relationship with Laurie just as she desired. For seventeen years, I was puzzled and mystified about the fact that he never admitted to me and possibly not even to himself that he might be the father of this illegitimate child. Over and over I reviewed in my mind that, in those years, he had been offered three separate opportunities to listen, honor, and respect me. I regurgitated that his response to the letter I sent while pregnant was to not respond. Over and over, I heard his response during our telephone conversation shortly after her birth, "This is all very interesting. I will pray for you and the child." And then again, I reviewed his response to the social worker when Laurie was a toddler, "I do not know this woman." I remembered the sweet, dapple-eyed social worker explaining about how Saul shared that many women students became infatuated with him and that I must be one of those women. I could only believe that he was lobbying for her to think of me as a crazed/delusional woman.

That phrase, "a crazed/delusional woman" haunted me for many years. I do not know if he ever said it. However, it was inferred by his comments to the social worker. I have wondered if I ever misrepresented him in a previous life. If so, I have forgiven myself many times and have asked him soul to soul to forgive me for such disrespectful behavior.

Laurie Longs to Know Her Father

For years I had been torn apart by Laurie's irreconcilable need to know her father. Part of me wanted to respect his wish to not be involved with us. My head and my emotions were stretched by strong pulls on either side. Laurie's desire and my promise to her were winning the struggle.

When we arrived in town, we went to the coffee shop next to Saul's store. The manager assured me that Saul came in a couple times a day. We must have waited for an hour and a half before he came in. With a smile, I invited him over to our table. Such being his memory, he did not recognize me from the meeting just three years earlier. Quivering with fear and attempting to smile nonthreateningly, I gently introduced myself and introduced him to Laurie. I said clearly to Laurie, "This is Saul Barodofsky."

Not waiting to build further rapport, I calmly told him that Laurie was his daughter and that she desired to know him. I said that I would like to talk more. He was leaden in his response: "I don't know you." He stood up and walked out of the café, zombielike.

I felt sorry for all of us! Laurie was startled by her father's abrupt disappearance. She seemed to be in a daze. She asked, "Where did he go?" I explained to her that he was surprised and did not know how to respond.

After my writing classmates heard me read this section in class, their faces dropped and they stared blankly for a few moments. Their real-life, down-to-earth, duality comments about this situation were very welcome to me fifteen years later. I had been brainwashed by the entire spiritual routine of-- "It's as it should be." I had filled myself with so much spiritual blah, blah that I didn't see objective facts clearly.

A published female writer my age said, "This is just a *guy* stuck in the 70s and into denial." To me she sounded refreshingly like a caring therapist. It was also a relief to hear a comment that I easily could have made about another woman in my situation.

I mentioned during an earlier class that I had just learned about sexsomnia and wondered if Saul suffered from that. For me, that possibly explained why he might not remember having sex with me. A female memoirist working for the Federal Government logically offered, "How old was he when you conceived?"

"He was 36. He did state, 'There will be no sex.' Maybe that was his way of warning me to take responsibility for his/our actions."

"He would have had to know by age 36 if he suffered from sexsomnia. His wives and other female partners would have given him feedback. If he was a responsible man, he would have respected your comments and taken responsibility for his possible actions. Anyway, a respectable man, let alone a spiritual teacher, would not walk away from a woman introducing him to his supposed child."

Speaking of responsibility! I remember distinctly that moment of announcing Saul's paternity to him in that coffee shop as the most outstanding relief from stress and pressure I have ever felt! I felt cleansed and responsible to myself and Laurie. I also experienced a feeling of equanimity. Finally, we three actors in my mystifying karma were at one table for at least three minutes. It was a cleansing experience for me after hiding the truth for so long. To this day, I am pleased that Laurie had this one opportunity to meet him, look into his eyes, and shake his hand.

I found it so confusing, frustrating, and discouraging that this strange man known internationally as a spiritual guide was so into denial or had such a horrific memory that he would not acknowledge me. I wondered again about how he could forget the scene: the cliff, the palm reading, the horrific rain. Anyway, here was a "guy," now middle aged, who did not remember me after counseling me, meditating with me, sheltering me from a storm, and then impregnating me in his Sufi Camp kiosk in 1975. His denial seemed like a hell of a storm to me. No shelter there! I puzzled then and have puzzled many times since then: What is my karma with him? What did I ever do to him?

I prayed internally. Forgive me, God, if I hurt him sometime. God, how do I help Laurie have a decent and real relationship with this man? And God, help me create positive karma with him or without him regarding this lesson. May I *never* have to deal with this aspect of a man's character again! May I never put a child or myself through this again! Amen!

When he left, he probably walked next door to his store. A few minutes later, I saw him, corpse-like, pass the coffee shop window with his briefcase. He disappeared up the street quickly. In fifteen minutes, I was in a state of peace and determination. I boldly walked Laurie next door.

It was common knowledge that Saul and his wife ran the store together. She was there. We introduced ourselves to Ananda, Saul's wife. I hoped that she would be my ideal of a Sufi woman: a problem solver, a woman of great honor, and respectful to other women. I prayed that she would be able to listen openly with trust. From what little I knew of his thinking, she probably had been prepared by him that a crazed/delusional woman was next door. I said, "I assume Saul told you we were next door." With a flat affect, she nodded. I quickly explained Laurie's parentage and that she longed for a relationship with her father. I stated that I hoped we could talk. She was coolly gracious, seemingly calm. She asked no questions and obviously did not want to discuss the topic. Possibly she was in shock. I have always imagined that she was praying and chanting internally, hoping I would disappear.

Laurie was immaculate, dressed in a navy blue dress with white polka dots with a matching hair band. She fawned over Ananda as she sat stoically on a wooden stool. Laurie hugged her, fondled her hair, and massaged her shoulders, obviously tense by this time. Ananda tolerated Laurie's touch and attention. She made sure she did not meld into Laurie's affection. She yielded enough to mention that she felt the strong power of healing in Laurie's hands. I concurred and shared that Pir Vilayat had given her the spiritual name Rafaeli when she was three months old. There was no need to explain to Ananda the meaning of Rafaeli. She would know this as a diminutive name for the Archangel of Healing. I wondered what she made of the connection that her husband was a healing leader and that I was claiming Laurie, a seventeen-year-old healer, was his daughter.

Laurie drank Ananda in and then explored the beauty of the store's Asian nomadic tribal woven merchandise. It was an exotic setting. Laurie was content that day to be in Saul's shop, to meet his wife, and to pet his dog. For years, Laurie talked joyfully about petting and knowing her father's dog.

During our visit, two thirty-something, tall men matched in height walked into the store. They softly murmured something to Ananda as they walked past her. They took up guard posts just behind her at the rear of the store. She greeted them with a nod and not more than a sentence. It was obvious that these men had been called to protect Ananda and to intimidate me. They never made eye contact with me. Laurie avoided them.

Laurie Longs to Know Her Father

From the corners of their eyes, the guards watched Laurie curiously as she explored the colorful merchandise. Ananda never asked me to leave. I am quite sure that I did not look or sound like someone after revenge. I was too stunned and shy to comment on the arrival of the sentries. I found the situation comical.

The men actually stood there mute and shoulder to shoulder. They reminded me of the young sentries always on duty at the Norwegian Royal Palace in Oslo. We would take a detour on our walking path to movies on Sunday so that Laurie could tease and flirt with those sentries. She always hoped to get a smile. Neither these Charlottesville sentries nor the Norwegian King's Guards smiled at Laurie!

Later, when I described these two store-cops to a friend, she thought that one of them fit the description of the regional leader of the local spiritual community. And if he was, I wondered why as a spiritual leader he did not care enough to question me. What was all this paranoia, suspicion, distrust? I wondered what strange power Saul held over people. Everyone seemed to be suspicious and to lose their humanity over this subject/conflict. Unfortunately for him, it was a conflict that Saul was aggravating. Of course, I was aggravating the conflict by just showing up. I realize that I am aggravating this conflict now as I share this story in openness. Surely, my Sufi women friends have encouraged me to expose this ancient, old-fashioned male domination of women and disregard for sired children.

I knew then that it was clear we would have to go into family court to prove paternity if there would be any chance of a relationship between Laurie and her biological father. I cringed, thinking that court procedures might escalate the "we are separate" game. I prayed that clarity and not hostility would be the outcome of the paternity test. My idealistic we-create-our-own-reality-self hoped that we could begin playing the "Laurie and Saul are family" game.

I told Ananda that I had hoped we could handle this privately. Because she and Saul obviously did not want to discuss our issues, my only recourse was to go to Family Court to prove paternity.

It was clear that I was a woman on a mission. Laurie and I graciously said goodbye.

11 Family Court

"What's the big deal? People have affairs.
Pregnancies happen. Babies are born. It's no big deal!"

~A younger male student/colleague of Saul

Duty-driven, we were a woman and a girl on a mission. Laurie and I walked the few blocks in the southern steamy weather to the family court building to file Laurie's case. I discovered that I needed a lawyer. I searched the yellow pages, chose one with powerful and idealistic numerology, called her office, and made an appointment for the next morning. When we met, she told me that Saul would be served with papers that very day. The next day, we sat in Family Court for two hours awaiting directives for the case. Two days later, we met in the judge's private chambers.

Thankfully, I picked a brilliant, objective, kind-hearted, female lawyer. Her voice, which resonated in her head and heart, assured me that she was a woman of integrity and mind/soul integration. The atmosphere in the room was chilly. Saul attempted to maintain authority in his tan, southern, summer suit. He put his Panama hat on the table. He then moved it to the floor because it obviously dominated the small round table. His lawyer, a matter-of-fact woman with a strident and heady voice, slammed folders around while huffing. Obviously, she believed that Saul did not know me. The judge, a forty-year-old, portly, handsome male, reportedly a gentleman cattle rancher, said in a broad Southern accent, "Aaaah—Mizzz Pippeenjaahr, would you aaah be willinn' —to paaay for the DEE EN AY testinn' if Miistaahr Baarahdofsky is naaht the faahther of your chaaild?"

In Northern speed, I chirped, "Most certainly!" My lawyer smiled. The judge jolted. Saul looked puzzled. His eyes flashed with fear. His lawyer glared at me. Her eyes froze momentarily on my grin. As I relive this moment, I think that grin was actually manifesting as a self-satisfied smirk! She glanced at my lawyer, who looked relaxed and contented. Then his lawyer, looking alternately angry and confused, snapped to attention with piercing eyes directed at Saul. And I felt my jaw set! I had had enough! I was tired of being ignored, dismissed, and disdained! I did not believe that I deserved this disrespect. In silence, I slipped into a female warrior mode. It stirred deeply inside me. In that moment, I suddenly felt like I was fighting for all women of all times and from everywhere! I was convinced that women did not deserve this disdain. And Sufi women definitely did not deserve to be shunned into submission and silence.

In issues of disharmony, my inclination is to apply forgiveness. I pray to create and find agreement quickly. So, regarding this emotion of dismissal I was experiencing, my prayer for many days was: "May those I have treated with disdain in any and all lifetimes forgive me. I forgive myself for anytime I have ignored, dismissed, and treated others with disdain! May I never do this to anyone ever again. May I create peace!" I observe myself closely and still struggle with the lesson as a perpetrator. I pondered for many months whether or not I was disdainful and disrespectful to Saul. After receiving reassurance to tell Laurie's entire story from my Buddhist teacher, Venerable Dagpo Rinpoche, I no longer puzzle over this. It does not fit for me, nor is it relevant.

What is relevant is the fact that being submissive and silencing the truth does not for wisdom make. Nor does silencing the truth serve Laurie in anyway.

Laurie and I were flying back to Norway the next day. The judge ordered our blood drawn in the United States to expedite the DNA testing. He arranged for us to rush to a court-approved laboratory several hours away in Fairfax, near our departing airport, Dulles International. The laboratory extended their hours to accommodate the judge. Our pictures were taken and our blood was drawn for the DNA test that very afternoon. The man drawing our blood wore a Mickey Mouse tie, which became legendary years later, when Laurie needed to have her blood drawn twice a year for testing her thyroid levels. Ever after, Laurie wanted every male medical technologist who drew her blood to have a Mickey Mouse tie. Silly me, I should have bought one and carried it along for all of her blood tests. In fact, I am buying the next one I see. Laurie is tested for thyroid checks two or more times a year.

Those days and often through the years, I have thought about the fact that Murshid Samuel Lewis, Saul's early Sufi teacher, was a gardener. It is common knowledge—he taught students that, if you plant a seed, you attend to it. He was an extreme teacher of responsibility. Vignettes and humorous anecdotes of his creative means of correcting students into recognizing responsibility abound.

I do not know what Murshid advised his male students regarding impregnating females with their human seeds. Certainly the state of Virginia was going with the theme that, if you "dip your wick" and sire a child, you care for that child.

I searched for reasons why I was in this karmic struggle. The psychic reading Paul Solomon gave me in 1977 said that Saul and I had planned to come into this life together. The reading explained that we had been together in many other lifetimes. It went on to say that, at the last minute, there was a decision that my soul could learn more by coming in without him. I always read into the message an inference that there was a contract to give Laurie her body from an earlier agreement. So she led us together on that flooded bridge to meet and create her body. I am convinced that I have had more learning opportunities without his (in my opinion) dominant presence.

Saul was born in 1939 and I was born in 1940; certainly we both were programmed with intellectual conditioning in our youth that men were stronger and that women should be, or should at least act, weaker. My mother literally told me to appear less intelligent than the men I dated and also to act weaker than I was. Unfortunately, I had been playing the weak and deficient person in this situation between us. With Family Court procedures assisting Laurie and me, there was a sense of possible equality.

For years, I had consciously been striving to express a greater balance of yin and yang energies in my activities and relationships. It was my desire to model that for my spiritual students. Mothering Laurie with her strong, willful, dominant presence had been serving me well to become forceful when appropriate. Living in Norway offered many examples of female role modeling and empowerment for this inner and outer work. Norway generally ranks as one of the top four leading countries in the yearly international gender equality listing. Living in a country with a high level of gender equality was deeply satisfying and rewarding.

I chuckled upon hearing a glamorous, aging token-wife from southern Europe humorously and disgustedly describe Norwegian women. She said that they can ski over the highest mountain, carry a basket of food they made for an ailing grandmother, stop and give birth on the way, continue protecting the baby from the cold, and finish their Ph.D. dissertation on their lap top while skiing. Norwegian women are generally well balanced. For centuries, Viking women ran their communities and homes when their men were at sea. They ran the businesses, the government, the schools, and their homes while remaining sexy and attractive. They developed balanced androgynous qualities as a result.

In modern times, they do not wear tailored little imitation men's suits as many professional American women do. Nor do they toddle precariously around on stilt heels, putting themselves at peril balance-wise. We can all recall scenes of models falling on runways. Norwegian women know that high heels do not give them power. They wear shoes with graceful heels that keep them as grounded and flexible as their male counterparts. They wear flowing, feminine, colorful clothing while seated in parliament. Norwegian men appreciate strong women. I appreciate Norwegian men and women for their respectful, sexually egalitarian culture. Certainly, the educated Norwegian men I knew did not have a chauvinistic remnant in their being.

As I struggled with my reason for having to deal with this lesson of approaching Saul to build a relationship with Laurie, I remembered a story. I had several past life memories before Laurie's birth, none of them related to Saul. I have probably had fifty past life memories during Laurie's lifetime. Only one memory includes him.

I remember being a Catholic mother in Ireland. I was married to a North Sea ship captain. We were a contented, prosperous, and well-respected family with seven children. A neighborhood boy joined my husband's crew and came back from his first voyage in shock. He reported to his mother that everyone on the crew knew and kept the secret that my husband had a second large family in the Netherlands. The boy had secretly trailed my husband to his Dutch home and observed the second family greeting him.

The boy's mother shared the news of the other family with me. I was shattered emotionally. I was so horrified, shamed, and distraught that I decided to end my life. In complete self-centeredness and without any thought of my children's future, I jumped from a cliff onto the rocky shore below, shattering my body. The children were devastated and felt abandoned. They were ashamed that their Catholic mother had committed suicide. I recall that one of the children, the soul I know now as Saul, was only seven years old.

This dramatic trauma might explain why Saul might subconsciously hold a payback attitude toward me. My selfish abandonment of the children could have created my need for the current lesson. After experiencing this memory, I attempted to heal its influence on my soul and forgave myself for abandoning the children. Heart-to-heart and soul-to-soul, I asked those beings who were my children then to forgive me. I also forgave the philandering husband, whom I thankfully have never encountered or recognized this lifetime.

God knows, I make a sincere effort and continually strive to correct as many parenting ills of myself and of my parents as I can. I do this in great hope and expectation that, by creating good parenting merit, I will deserve fabulous parenting in future lifetimes. I hope to deserve great, attentive parents who are healthy in all aspects.

My parents this lifetime were attentive, caring, and committed to my happiness and education. As a couple, they were role models of immaturity and hatred. Saul and I were embroiled in what I labeled great immaturity, and he certainly resented my persistence.

Over several months, Saul's lawyer delayed the Family Court process with myriad excuses. She whined about being pressed for time. It was also obvious to the judge and my lawyer that she was attempting to wear me down financially and energetically. At a crucial point, the judge demanded that they get court-required information together before I left town to prevent me from making yet another trip from Norway. I made a total of three trips. The last one was after the results of the blood test proved with 99.98% accuracy that Saul was Laurie's father. My lawyer had expressed concern, because a positive test as low as 92% can be thrown out of court. Because Laurie's coloring, hair, and temperament are more like Saul's than mine, I had anticipated a high DNA result. My lawyer and I were elated with the results. Finally, there was proof! Now, if we could just build a relationship between Saul and Laurie.

Saul appeared bewildered with the test results. It appeared that he really did not know that he "knew" me! I informed the judge that the purpose of the procedures was to establish proof of paternity and then to work on establishing a relationship between Laurie and her father. I was not asking for a money settlement. He suggested mediation.

I had spent a total of $9,000 on the three trips. Expenses included flights, Laurie's care, the lawyer, motels, food, and rental cars to make Laurie's dream come true. I did want my expenses covered. However, the judge and tradition determined there would be a monetary settlement only for Laurie's use. I was responsible for my expenses. The judge ordered Saul to pay for the DNA test and a $16,000 one-time payment for Laurie's lifetime support. Both American and European friends found the judge's decision outrageous. I did not contest it; receiving support for Laurie had not been our objective. Our objective was to establish a blissful father-daughter relationship between Laurie and her biological father, Saul.

Mediation was arranged. The judge suggested that this expense be split, and it was. In the first session, Saul and I were alone with the mediator. He opened up more than I expected. He shared that his father left his mother when he was two years old. "Murshid Sam was like a father to me. He is really the only father I have known." Throughout the years, those simple sentences have left me wondering about, and I admit, judging his choices. I've asked myself several times: *Does he ever consider gathering good-father-merit this lifetime in order to deserve an open, balanced, flexible, respectful, vibrant man as a father next lifetime?*

Soon, in a disdainful, sing-song tone I heard, "You should have gotten an abortion. Why would you **even consider** having a baby from a one night stand?" My family therapist training knew by this mocking intonation that he was not interested in any answer. This was not Saul's Sufi healer/counselor voice.

Because of the DNA test result, he could no longer classify me as a crazed/delusional woman. Now, it seemed he was attempting to classify me as a 70s-dumb-blonde-bimbo. With eighteen years of proof that he was not fond of my sharing anything regarding the pregnancy, I simply said, "I had wanted a child for years and it seemed foolish to abort this accidental pregnancy." My sympathetic-to-Buddhism values about the difficulty of obtaining a body for rebirth, etc., I did not bother to share. He never asked about my background and experiences. It seemed like, the less he knew about us, the better for him. It was obvious that he was not interested in knowing that I was also a world-traveled spiritual teacher who guided students in several countries and who might have thoughts about our karma together and how we could reach a state of grace and beauty. His cup seemed full of himself; I believed there was no room for input.

Because our history included my feeling of being disrespected, I did not tell Saul that I knew Laurie was the incarnation or an incarnation of Murshid Sam or that I thought it was spiritually and personally unfortunate for him to reject her. I was not throwing any pearls out to him yet. Surely, he would scoff. I was still hoping that he would choose to have experiences with Laurie that would allow him to be blessed personally by her touch and remarkable wisdom.

This lack of fathering of both Saul and Murshid Sam intrigues and puzzles me. Murshid Sam's father ignored him as much as possible, even though it was obvious that his son was a prodigy. I find it especially intriguing, because I believe Laurie expresses the soul of Murshid Samuel Lewis. Here, Sam, as Laurie, again has a father who ignores him.

I read a recent book by Mansur Johnson, who was a disciple of Murshid. The book is entitled, *Murshid, A Personal Memoir of Life with American Sufi Samuel L. Lewis.* Another disciple, Murshid Wali Ali Meyer, wrote the introduction, in which he quotes Sam: "My parents never forgave me for being conceived out of wedlock." That is quite understandable, in that it must have been terribly embarrassing in that time and in that place. Samuel Lewis's conception was in early 1896 San Francisco society; his parents were Jacob Lewis, a vice-president of the Levi Strauss Company, and Harriet Rothschild, of the international banking family.

In the mediation sessions, it seemed to me that Laurie's father was not about to forgive her for being conceived out of wedlock this lifetime. Nor was he forgiving me, the bimbo, for choosing to give birth to her.

The following day, Ananda joined us for the second session. It was quickly evident when they entered that they had decided they did not have room in their lives for Laurie and that they were not willing to reconsider and make room for Laurie. I felt like I was watching a scene from a soap opera with a cooing couple.

With gentle eye contact between them, Ananda to Saul, "Don't you think we are parenting enough children?"

"Well, I suppose we really are. There is… and…"

"Yes, and that is time-consuming with your travel, responsibilities, and the store."

I sputtered, "You do not need to parent her. I do that. What about an occasional short visit? Could we just be friends? Laurie only wants to know you."

Looking at each other rather simultaneously, they said, "No, we are not interested in a friendship."

Momentarily, my heart sank in disbelief. Internally I heard myself think, "Dear God, I have come this far, and this is a standoff!?" Still feeling strong and calm, I digested the news. They did not want to spend time with Laurie. Just two or three days a year would have been a wonderful solution for Laurie. They refused the offer to build harmony and to create a friendship with us. The seed of his loin was not going to know her sire.

They did, however, make a point to go out of their way to praise me for doing such a great job of raising Laurie. I thanked them. They thought she functioned admirably as a Down syndrome person. (I am quite sure they did not know that she was "mosaic" and high functioning.) They wanted me to know they recognized that I was a great parent. Yes, I thought, but Laurie wants two great parents. Obviously, they had decided Saul was not going to be one of them.

I also thought of the words of the itinerant Jewish teacher of two thousand years ago, "As you do unto the least of these, you do unto me." In this case, Laurie as the less-fortunate Down syndrome child was rejected, and Laurie the unknown, Sufi mystic and master healer, was also rejected.

One of my greatest hurts and longest-running negative emotions from this saga is the lack of consideration of my merit as a person. This, of course, has to do with my personal ego weakness. I actually cared whether they thought I was a bimbo or not. I imagined two spiritual people in this situation would have considered our lifestyle and would be open to sharing ideals, goals, and intentions. They never seemed to flirt with the idea that a friendship with us might add beauty and blessings to their lives.

In a continued self-protective fighting mode, Saul made sure the court agreement stated that I was not to ask for money again. That seemed strangely bizarre to me, because I was not after money. It reads that if I ask for money, I would have to return the $16,000 awarded to Laurie. Duality games over sex, money, and power are rampant on this dear planet. Laurie's operetta had been a battleground of all three topics. Money fears seemed to be at the forefront of this particular decision.

With all of the talk of healthcare that I hear daily as I finish this book, I realize that they might have feared that Laurie was a sieve for medical costs. They did not know that Laurie was totally healthy and had never needed surgery.

Thankfully, I have never been (and may I never be) swamped with medical bills. Plus, we lived in Norway, where everyone is protected by national insurance. Possibly they thought that Laurie had an unfortunate trisomy 21 condition and might need numerous heart surgeries. Laurie has been hospitalized only once for one day with the swollen tongue incident.

Saul read the mediation agreement as if we were not to have any contact ever again. I did not understand the agreement to say that we could not say hello if we met on the street or at a gathering. After all, we were civil in mediation. No one raised their voice once.

Many friends have repeated through the years that it is Saul's loss for not knowing Laurie. To me, it is amusing and intriguing that many cognitively impaired people walk past Saul's store—at least, they did in 1994. A waitress at the coffee shop confirmed there was an adult employment program nearby. Several Down syndrome people walk past his store Monday through Friday. Even though he may choose to not know Laurie, is he able to forget her?

Remember the Social Services office in Woodstock, Virginia? After the DNA testing, I felt an obligation and duty to other young women to talk with them. I also could not resist stopping by with an "I told you so!" and a reprimand that I thought they deserved. Standing at a counter with the receptionist, I asked if the woman who had handled my case was available. I announced that I wanted to show her the DNA test results and suggest she not dismiss women as easily as she dismissed me. "Oh, those records would have been purged. Yes, she works here. She's not here. She is out in the field today."

I, sternly, loudly, and self-righteously suggested that the social workers listen more closely and respectfully to women's stories and be less affected by the charm of men! I was quickly dismissed again by the office manager. There was no apology, although the director of the office came out as I was walking away and respectfully thanked me for my message. I interpreted that as confirmation that she had felt some regret about the poor handling of Laurie's case and the fifteen years of lost time. Her thank you saved her agency from receiving a raving letter from me to the editor of the local newspaper and to the state executive of social work agencies.

I am grateful for the friend who advised me to go to family court. It is a great assurance there is DNA testing now for other children and mothers facing the situation with "wayward fathers." And I hope that all young mothers in similar situations have family and community support to get to a family court for DNA testing for closure, for self-respect, and for the benefit of their children. Laurie was not allowed to have her father listed on her birth certificate at birth. I have not yet submitted the copy of the DNA test to get a new birth certificate for her. It will be good to bring that bit to closure. She will feel more complete with Saul's name on her birth certificate.

12 Tell Them About My Father!

"…people tell themselves that if it [a secret] isn't talked about, it doesn't exist. This simply does not work, ever, unless everyone you are 'protecting' is mute, deaf, and blind."

~ from The New Peoplemaking by Virginia Satir

Once or twice a year, Laurie has begged me to arrange a meeting with Saul. I have finally convinced her that he does not want an earthly relationship with us. She has stopped asking, although she says every two or three months that "I wish my father wanted to know me." She mentions at least once a month that she wants to know her half-brother and -sister. My heart pangs momentarily each time she asks. And then I let it go. This is her karma. The master in her needs to solve it.

Laurie's half-sister and I did enjoy one delightful half-hour telephone call. A mutual friend, who is an old family friend, gave me her number without asking permission. So the call was unexpected. I hemmed and hawed and then finally managed to tell Laurie's sister the purpose of the call. She was in shock. It was not entirely surprising to me that her father never informed her or her brother that they had a half-sister. I told her it seemed obvious to me that Saul maintained a secretive system around him.

I shared that I agree with the Virginia Satir and the Edgar Cayce philosophies: Everybody really knows what is going on, so you might as well bring it out in the open and talk about it. Cayce maintained that everyone dreams about everything before it happens. As we talked, I remembered thinking that Saul's attitude and Paul Solomon's attitude of secretiveness are the antithesis of Peace Through Understanding, my life's work.

After five minutes of recovery from her shock, Saul's daughter from his first marriage expressed loving sincerity. I apologized to her for having a one-night stand with her father when he was married to her mother. (Later, I actually understood that is was while he was married to his second wife.) His daughter graciously accepted my apology. She even expressed being pleased that "something good" had come out of the sleeping around of the 1970s.

She expressed excitement about having a sister and wanted to meet Laurie. We talked excitedly about the possibilities and arranged a date to meet in two weeks. We live more than three hundred fifty miles apart. I was relieved with this open, spontaneous contact and was very willing to drive to her community.

In that half-hour telephone conversation, we did a Reader's Digest summary of Laurie's life and of her sister's life and relationship with her father. I rattled off details as fast as I could. I explained that Laurie's private middle school teacher and Oslo's guidance counselor decided that Laurie was to be trained in textile arts and crafts at Sandaker High School in Oslo. She specialized in patchwork sewing and worked as part of her training at Balders Textile in Frogner. I described the elegant converted home, with Italian sculpted plaster ceilings, crystal chandeliers, and a warm and inviting atmosphere. The staff was and is delightful, and the walls are painted a cheerful lemon chiffon. I explained that, in the summer when Laurie graduated, as other staff and workers vacationed, she was left alone with one staff member for a month who taught her to weave. I proudly said, "Laurie has been a weaver since that time, and she is employed at a cottage industry here in our community."

Both Laurie's half-sister and I were astonished that both sisters are weavers by profession. We laughed that weaving must be in their genes. Laurie's half-sister runs a weaving studio for women who are disenfranchised. Their father is known as a weaving scholar.

I shared that I found it eerie and amusing that both Saul and Laurie presented at the Textile Museum, part of the Smithsonian Museum system in Washington, DC, once a year. He lectures there about once a year as an expert on nomadic rugs. Laurie's cottage industry always asks her to demonstrate weaving for an hour or two on the family event days in June. (The past three years, Laurie has refused to demonstrate at the Textile Museum on family days. That vague line of connection between them is severed.)

Laurie's half-sister shared warmly and openly. We laughed and sighed a lot. She laughed when I asked, "Do you have good, strong teeth?"

"Yes, I've never had a cavity." Laurie has never had a cavity. Impenetrable teeth seem to run in their family! Secretly, I hoped impenetrable hearts did not run in the family.

I had not told Laurie that I was calling her sister in case of rejection and denial. I did not want her to face rejection by another member of the family. Gathering courage, I had held off calling for several weeks. I was waiting for all of the holiday activities to come to a close, waiting for a propitious aspect of the moon, and waiting until I felt grounded.

When I got off the phone, I was so excited that Laurie was accepted! Going straight to Laurie's room, I bubbled over, "I just talked to your sister. She wants to meet you. Isn't that fabulous? We are going to meet her soon. Guess what? She's a weaver too! We will drive to her home. She has a son. You have a nephew." Jumping and laughing, Laurie was obviously thrilled and asked more questions. We hugged, laughed, and cried, and I started to plan the trip.

Something came up, and I called back a week later to rearrange the meeting. Her husband answered the phone and said the meeting was not possible. He said that "family members" (Ananda and Saul, I assume) convinced Laurie's sister that it was not a good idea. When I called the mutual friend to ask if she could understand this change of heart, she reported she had heard that the chit-chat was that "we were only after money." I was shocked, angry, and disappointed. I could not understand this betrayal and distortion of truth. What a terrible task it was to inform Laurie that her dream of knowing her half-sister was shattered.

When I told Laurie that her half-sister did not want to meet her now because the rest of the family thought we were only after money, Laurie spurted out in her mastery, *"It's her business, not theirs! Tell her that! It's her business, not theirs!"* Regrettably, I could not tell her. I no longer had access. Hopefully, she will come to that conclusion herself before she and Laurie are in their eighties. I am so sorry now that I did not allow Laurie to say hello to her sister during the joyful conversation. That might have been her last chance to talk with her.

Tell Them About My Father!

May Laurie's half siblings truly understand someday that our intention was (and is):

1. to get a relationship established;
2. for Laurie to have a sense of a joyous, harmonious, respectful, open family relationship;
3. to explore her roots and heritage; and
4. to obtain a family health history. It was the judge's suggestion that Saul provide that to me. To this date, it has not been delivered.

I am convinced that the two sisters would relish each other and would enjoy sharing weaving ideas and patterns. Laurie also wants to meet her big brother and Saul's grandchildren. Unfortunately this family, even though grounded in hippie philosophy from the 1970s, has decided not to share an extended family and loving community with us. Of course, that is their right. Laurie is dealing with the loss.

The myth that we are "only after money" reappeared when Laurie's Social Security worker insisted that I notify Social Security when Saul retired. The worker told me to make sure that Saul filed for Laurie's Social Security adult disabled child payments. Unfortunately, I did not hire a lawyer to do this. The worker told me that he could not make the call. I bolstered myself and prayed for understanding during my preparation for making the call. Then I called the Sunday after Saul's birthday of eligibility. I knew that he would apply for his pension precisely on time. He spat out, "I already filed this week!"

I smiled and thought, *Yup. His astrological stellium of five planets in Capricorn* [in our few brief meetings, he had mentioned this aspect of his astrological chart twice] *was predictable. He's precisely on time!*

He continued to rage, yelling that he knew nothing about a disabled child form. "I'm not going back to that office, and I'm not filling it out!" My chest quaked. I felt violated from the blast of his fury. I said thank you, hung up, and prayed prayers of peace for him and prayers of protection for Laurie and me.

Possibly he thought I was after money from him personally. A student of his and a friend of ours, Hadiya (name changed), had called him earlier that very morning, unbeknownst to me. She wished him happy birthday and then she beseeched him to fill out Social Security forms to ensure that Laurie would receive the monthly stipend she was due on his retirement. I can surmise that Saul became infuriated when he discovered that Hadiya knew about Laurie and when she spoke to him on Laurie's behalf.

As we talked later in the day, Hadiya expressed concern about her student relationship with him. I was so brainwashed by Paul Solomon's version of the English spiritual tradition that students should not know about weaknesses of their spiritual teacher that I felt a twinge of guilt. Oh, my God, I thought, "My revelation has hurt her relationship to her spiritual guide." I then jolted in another direction. Buddhist literature suggests that, before choosing a Buddhist teacher, you should know of his/her history for twelve years. This is to assure you that the teacher is of moral character in all aspects of his/her life. I only knew Saul's title for a few hours before conceiving his child. I do not know how long she knew him before choosing him as her spiritual guide.

Following is how Hadiya and I became friends: We met at a Dances of Universal Peace seminar. At first glance, she felt and looked like a sister to me. We enjoyed each other and quickly became friends, squeezing time in our busy schedules to see each other. This woman loves Murshid Sam and Sufi stories. She also delighted in meeting Laurie. As an artist she admired Laurie's sewing and weaving projects. Hadiya was an active Sufi student. She shared that she drove several hours to Charlottesville from Fairfax, Virginia, for a monthly teaching session with Saul Barodofsky. I gulped and thought, "Do I reveal my secret and share our story with her?"

It took me weeks of soul searching, meditation, and prayer to open up to her. Finally, I shared, "Laurie is Saul's daughter. I went to Family Court and there is DNA proof. He does not want any contact with her. Plus, I have a myriad reasons that I will share with you why I think Laurie is an incarnation/expression of Murshid Sam."

Bless Hadiya, she was open and made no judgment. That day, she had bought and delivered a stuffed animal to Laurie that had another animal peeking out of its mouth. She shared that she was not attracted to it, but felt driven and compelled to buy it. She was shocked when I then confided the reasons I thought Laurie was expressing Murshid Sam's soul. She understood the symbol of the gift she had purchased earlier in the day—Sam was peeking out of Laurie's mouth.

On Monday, I called Laurie's Social Security advisor and told him that her father refused to file the form. "Is Mr. Barodofsky's social security number in Laurie's file?" I assured him that it was in the DNA file. He responded, "Good, then I can arrange Laurie's disabled child pension now that I know he has filed for his own Social Security." And so it was done. With nothing coming from Saul's personal pocket, every month a United States "pension" check for his disabled child is deposited into an account for Laurie. It is small and it will stop if and when she might become self-sufficient or wealthy.

I know that this story is divinely perfect, yet I judge and wonder, "How can I have this karma with a spiritual teacher? He surely knows and teaches the universal laws of cause and effect and yet expresses so little interest in his child." Especially, I wonder this because he was abandoned at two. As Laurie would say, his part of it is none of my business. Is all of this seemingly irresponsible behavior really from the wisdom of his heart, offered purely to teach me a lesson? It often feels like a kind of revenge that has little to do with me. All of my spiritual friends would say, "Yes, he's your teacher!" Surely, I know that. Paul Solomon would have said that to me, and I would say the same to anyone I coached in this predicament: "He is a wise man bearing you a gift." And he certainly bore me a gift: the right to parent a compassionate, wise being. And, often too mother-like, I think, "Poor Saul, you are missing a valuable person in this daughter."

In 1991 in the Netherlands, Atum O'Kane said, "I think The Dances of Universal Peace would be good for you." I did not ask why and registered the advice. The original dances had been created by Murshid Sam, and I thought they would be good to help me understand Laurie. Twelve years after the suggestion, while in the Washington, DC, area, I began studying The Dances of Universal Peace with Kathryn Ashera Rose as my mentor.

In our second session, I blurted, "I've got to share with you why I disappeared from the dances and the U.S. Sufi Order for 26 years!" Kathryn Ashera had met Laurie earlier at a dance gathering. I gave her "My Cosmic C-Movie" story. Kathryn Ashera expressed compassion for our plight. Kathryn Ashera urged me to tell the story within the Sufi community and to bring it out into the open. "American Sufi women are telling their stories. They have decided the men should not be protected from their indiscretions any longer." So, I continued with this advice and Laurie's directive to "Tell Them about My Father."

Tell Them About My Father!

Soon after this, I joined classes at the Baraka Center in Chevy Chase, MD. There, a woman's group led by Zarifah (Nancy) Kadian heard my story. They were appalled. This sisterhood encouraged me to be open and to stop hiding Laurie's parentage. "Laurie deserves to be known for who she is." All the Sufi women with whom I've talked are of the same mindset. It is time for transparency. It is time for men to be held responsible for their actions. It was a relief to share our story with them. It is a relief to put it on paper here.

On three continents for twenty-plus years, I traveled and revealed the fact that I was a spiritual guide/single mother with a special needs child from a one-night stand. That information seldom brought any discord or judgment. In hindsight, I see that it worked wonders. Most students respected me yet kept me off of an unnecessary pedestal.

I often pondered, "Why should a male spiritual teacher be protected from view, when a female spiritual teacher cannot be protected from an error of karma? Why had women been protecting men for thousands of years?" I have led hundreds of women through past life memories. I know that many of us have been bullied and brutalized into submission and silence by male domination. I know that, at deep cellular levels, we still fear beatings, burnings, dark powers, and shunning. When will that end?" Goodness knows that I had created my own shunning by disappearing from Sufi activities for years.

In a 2004 Dance Camp held in Charlottesville, Kathryn Ashera heard Ananda co-led a woman's group during which participants were encouraged to teach men by becoming examples of peace. The message was to teach men to heal old rifts and create peaceful relationships. That evening, Kathryn Ashera arranged a mediation session in which she confronted Ananda to heal and mend the situation with Laurie and me. When I heard about this, I was touched and humbled by her courageous action. I am quite sure this was the first time that Ananda and Saul learned that Laurie and I no longer lived in Norway. We had been back in the states for six years.

Friends encouraged me to attend this same popular regional Dance Camp in 2005. They exclaimed how wonderful it was. I decided to end my personal shunning and to show up at the same place as Saul. I knew that he was teaching two sessions late in the weekend. I questioned whether I should attend the camp for several weeks. Then, boldly and realistically, I thought, *I stayed out of his face and didn't show up for 28 years. I can show up now. If he doesn't like it, he can disappear for the next 28 years*!

I chose to stay off campus in a motel with a dear friend so that I could get the camp out of my senses and my system during the night. That decision provided much-needed privacy and saved me from dormitory chit chat. A mutual friend saw me early in the camp and alerted Saul and Ananda that I was in attendance. Ananda hugged me after the Friday evening session she led. She certainly did not work actively to "heal the relationship." I avoided Saul on Saturday and purposely left the venue when he was to teach. As I was leaving, he drove up early and walked past me. Not surprisingly, he did not recognize me.

My friends conveniently—although unplanned—sat around me and provided a shield of empathy during his Sunday morning healing service. He talked dramatically about healing all rifts, personal and political. He led the group in prayers and meditation for world peace and the ending of wars. When he was gathering his paraphernalia afterward, I dared to approach him. I could not imagine a more propitious time to create peace through understanding between us. I smiled and, with my head bent in a respectful Buddhist style, gently and softly said, "Laurie sends her warm greetings to you."

Like "The Incredible Hulk," he transformed and began to look furious and frazzled. He yelled, "Get away from me! You are never to talk to me! We have a court agreement!" Students around him looked puzzled. They were obviously concerned. It must have been shocking, because he had just led one hundred–plus people in prayer for "peace, harmony, and understanding" amongst all people everywhere, all enemies, and all nations. Forgive my Scorpio humor, but I did not seem to fit into any of these categories!

At that moment, with fear and rage distorting his face, I found him a pitiful, comic figure. Maybe this was a second moment of equalizing between our soul expressions on earth. I was coming into my personal rightful power. Was this what Paul's message meant, that I had much to learn by coming into this lifetime without Saul? And I have often wondered, had I and why would I spend lifetimes with this soul who now seemed so impenetrable and disrespectful? And why can't I remember them? Later that evening in meditation, I forgave myself for any and all times that I had been impenetrable.

As he turned his back, I moved as gracefully, graciously, and as quickly as I could to the back of the room to avoid antagonizing him more. I was quickly surrounded by supportive friends from the dance network who had observed his incongruous performance. The room was packed shoulder to shoulder in preparation for other activities. Several of Saul's students followed me and inched in to eavesdrop on our conversation, trying to get some understanding of the scene they had witnessed. I know at that time that he had not announced his illegitimate child to his students. In fact, as mentioned earlier, I understand that he has not acknowledged Laurie to his students. Friends ask me often, "Do you think his denial is because she is Down syndrome or because she is illegitimate?" I do not know. I hope and assume it is only the illegitimacy of her birth.

It's been eighteen years since the DNA testing occurred. I imagined by now that he would let this secret of fathering a special child with an adult student come to the light of day and just be objective fact. Why keep it a secret and let it smack of a scandal? As friends pointed out, Laurie is not listed on his Web page with his two children from a previous marriage. I cannot imagine why he fears announcing Laurie's presence. Once or twice a year, I impishly think about paying for a very late birth announcement in his local newspaper. I do agree with the Sufi women's group: "Laurie deserves to be known for who she is."

Within weeks after Laurie had screamed to me that she thought I had killed her father, I calmly called two Sufi leaders, both students of Murshid Sam and spiritual brothers of her father, to ask for their advice. I hoped they would be helpful. This was before DNA testing was common, so, of course, they had no idea if I was a deranged female or not. Unfortunately, they did the male dismissal thing, offering no suggestions or empathy. I understand that their hands were tied. However, their lack of expressed concern and coaching was disturbing. In both cases, I sensed that they wanted me off the phone as soon as possible. Their responses certainly did not welcome me back into the Sufi community. Only Atum O'Kane, with gentleness and kindness, in Switzerland welcomed me back into his classes, the Sufi community, and the teachings. This was years before the DNA testing was done.

Most of the male Sufi teachers who studied with Saul under Murshid Samuel Lewis have come to Washington DC in the past few years to teach workshops. They have been gracious as I have introduced them to Laurie and explained the DNA test results. That news, I think, traveled quickly within the leadership circle after I told my story in 2003. These revered teachers have individually welcomed Laurie into the community when I have presented her. Most have acknowledged that they sense her powerful healing energies. I hoped that they could bridge the gap for Laurie so that the dream of knowing her father and siblings could come true. When Pir Shabda Kahn came to DC in 2006, he knew of Laurie. He told me that he had worked to heal the divide between Saul and me. I am humbly grateful for his transparency and effort.

As mentioned earlier, I find it unfortunate that the extent of Laurie's relationship with her biological father has been shaking his hand one time in the coffee shop, being able to touch and hug his second wife a few moments, exploring his store, and getting to pet the family dog. No wonder she longed for her father. No wonder she longs for her roots.

An astrologer friend, out of curiosity, asked to look at Laurie's chart when I said that her father had boasted about having his rising sign and four planets in Capricorn. This configuration, called a stellium, in Capricorn represents strong doing-energy. The astrologer was enthralled with the analysis of their astrological connections. "There is no separation between Laurie and her father! They are one. They are working together in the ethers. They are in constant cosmic contact." Even though all of that was beyond my simple astrological understanding, it's not beyond simple Cosmology. According to her, Saul and Laurie are equal partners in spiritual action and wisdom in the Cosmos. I am reassured that maybe Laurie does not really need him as an earthly father if they work cosmically in consort. How is that for "hooga-booga?"

On the spiritual side of Oneness, I truly believe that there is "no blame." I also believe that the three of us—Laurie, her father, and me—or the six of us, adding Ananda and his two legal children, are one at a soul and cosmic level. Life is indeed an apparition. Laurie and I deserve this karma, or we have chosen to live it to present a teaching. Ultimately, there is no right and wrong or black and white. I have come to two conclusions: There is what creates fortunate karma or unfortunate karma. Hopefully, everyone in this Earthly Theater will ultimately choose fortunate karma and prevent future drama traumas. And, there is only what works and what does not work for people.

What works for me now is to release my promise to Laurie. I have made it clear to Laurie: "I am sorry. Forgive me. I have done everything I know of to get you a relationship to your father. It is up to you to work your magic."

It works to announce Laurie's place in the world by revealing her character, talents, spiritual lineage, and physical ancestry.

It works for me to claim my strength and equality with a dominant male spiritual teacher, to unveil this secret and its effect on Laurie and our community. Teaching open communications and practicing secrecy has been a disconnect for my students and for me. I hope that my students accept my apology for living a double standard and for not practicing what I preached.

It works for me to bless Saul and his family and his holy work.

It also worked for me recently to ask Laurie why she chose her father. She put her right hand gently over her heart in true Sufi fashion and said softly, "He is very wise inside his heart." She noticed that I stiffened ever so slightly and, looking me straight in the eyes, continued, "He reeeeally is. He knows that. I know that. God knows that. That's why I chose him."

13 Less-Than-Perfect Material

"When we do the best that we can, we never know what miracle is wrought in our life, or in the life of another."

~Helen Keller

When Laurie was an infant, Paul Solomon told me that she had been a master healer in many lifetimes. When she was a toddler, he told me that she had been a frustrated healer in many lifetimes. Many patients, clients, or students had not understood or believed her teachings. Paul continued, "Believe me, Laurie's Down syndrome diagnosis is no accident! Laurie came into this lifetime to personally demonstrate that you can come into a lifetime with less-than-perfect material and accomplish great things."

Laurie has used her "less-than-perfect material" to accomplish simple tasks. I hope this chapter empowers parents and caretakers of special needs children to go beyond the myths of diagnosis and to know much can be done to create a full and meaningful life. Laurie's mission continues to fascinate, amuse, and amaze me. She is attracted to people who live successful and noble lives from the role as seeming underdogs.

I assume that Laurie chose me as a parent in this lifetime because she trusted me to empower her to an enhanced potential. If she had been observing me from the ethers, she knew that my most joyful and fulfilling moments are when I successfully coach someone to reach their potential and/or to understand and resolve a repetitive soul lesson. I surmise that she knew I would not let her get away with slacking off and would persistently keep her in the moment. Many people with Down syndrome seem to spend a great deal of time drifting off into the ethers. Laurie has very often been nudged back into the "here and now" by her annoyed and annoying mother.

The most difficult aspect of raising Laurie was deciding when and when not to push her into learning a new skill or into new experiences. She learned to ride a short bicycle without training wheels. I knew that she would be able to ride a larger bicycle without training wheels. She was scared. She rode into a pole less than three feet away from the edge of a canal on her first trial as we left the posh bicycle shop. She refused to ride and screamed to me, "I'm never going to ride. I'm not riding! I'm not riding! You can't make me! I'm not riding!" I walked her new bike the 15 minutes to our home.

I had just spent several hundred guilders (then over $250 U.S.) on a gleaming five-speed Peugeot. I chose one that she would be able to ride for several years. I was furious. She was expressing her Aires sun stubbornness, her Taurus rising stubbornness, and her Down syndrome stubbornness. I knew that I would have to get even more stubborn to win this dragon fight. And I am not proud about how I did it. I expressed my anger on the following weekend. I offered to take her to the park, where there would be no poles and no canals. She refused three times. On the third refusal, I turned into a raging monster. I called her decision stupid. That was the first time that I used that word with her. She was shocked! In fact, so was I. But I was so very furious because I had just spent—really, sacrificed—all that money on a bike that she stated she was not going to ride.

My Name Is Laurie

I have only used the word stupid on very select occasions with her in the years since this incident. It definitely gets her attention, and I feel like there is a huge kneading fist in the pit of my solar plexus when I say it. But I do use it purposely on those few occasions.

I screamed and ranted like all the parents whom I judge to be bad parents. "Laurie, this is just stupid, really stupid to decide not to use this bicycle. And, I don't like that! It's stupid to think you can't learn to ride. It's stupid not to try. And you are too smart to do something so stupid! Of course, you can ride. Now, come to the park with me and I'll teach you to ride. Everyone in Holland rides a bike, and by God, you are going to ride!"

With less-than-perfect material and a much less-than-perfect mother, she grudgingly walked her gleaming bike to the park. In ten minutes, she learned to ride that fabulous, sleek, silver and white Peugeot! We rode our bikes almost every day that we lived in The Hague. My bike, by the way, was an aged maroon bent clunker. I bought it for five guilders and spent twenty getting it repaired. We were quite a disparate pair!

Laurie learned all of the traffic rules quickly. She had an increased sense of power on her bike. She really enjoyed bossing car drivers. They do not have the right of way at right turn intersections if a bike is present. She would look for them and scream, "Pas Op!" (Watch out!) and jut her palm up and out police-like at them if they looked like they might dare to cut her off! If they moved a foot toward her, she would shake her fist and scream "Pas Op!" more emphatically.

As mentioned earlier, Laurie has little tolerance for making errors. As a result, Laurie would often "pretend" or believe that she could not/would not learn something. I am sorry that I did not take more notes about the many specifics. On the one hand, she adores letting people know how much she adores them on paper and on the other hand, she dislikes writing notes and letters because she knows her spelling has many errors. Expecting first-time perfection is a hard line for anybody and especially for someone with cognitive disabilities.

During the years, there were many incidents during which I had to trust my intuition and gut feeling to decide how to empower her or whether I should just let her escape an opportunity for learning. I had to ask myself often: *Is this an appropriate lesson or task to teach her and/or do I let her zone out and pass on this?* I was often puzzled with this question when Laurie was between the ages of four and sixteen. This issue came up at least once a month. The decision to push or to leave her to her own designs was the issue. Often, it felt like a moral issue to me. Many days I wondered: *Am I being cruel or am I being helpful to push her? Do I insist that she learn this task?*

Most often, I pushed her. If I made the wrong choice and the task was too hard, I apologized. We hugged, often crying, and I was forgiven. Our mutual successes were wonderful. Now, as an adult she makes the decisions on her own to learn or not to learn and uses me and others as backup sources of information.

One of my prayers has been, *Oh, Dear God, don't let me mess her up!* I believe souls can regress and lose merit. Being in any way responsible for a soul regressing in merit is very unfortunate karma according to Hindu and Buddhist teachings. Like many people her age, she refuses to go to religious services unless I do a "this is a family-holy-day togetherness" plea. Occasionally, she has agreed to go to a Buddhist teaching in the Netherlands with Dagpo Rinpoche. Often she says to me in conversation, "I already asked God about…" She seems to be in prayer most of the day, even when glued to a television set. She often states, "I have God inside me every day. God is right here [pointing to her heart]. I have the Holy Spirit inside me. I don't need to go to church!"

She agreed to join me for a Universal Worship Service on Easter 2005. It was held in a private home. Many people participated in the presentation of readings and music from seven religions of the world. Laurie was not on the program. As soon as the service began, I could sense that she wanted to be involved. It was as if there was a powerful energy that surrounded her and filled her. She began to look like she was buzzing. (When this happens, it seems she must express or explode with energy. It is obvious to me that she is being guided.) I had hoped that she would offer to dance. However, she asked for permission to speak. She moved to the front of the room and took a self-assured position. She talked about love and service for three or four minutes, moving several people to tears.

I chose to forget this incident and Susanna McIlwaine reminded me and imitated Laurie. Laurie stood there with one hand pointed at heaven and the other hand directed at earth. Then Laurie made a sweeping gesture in my direction and announced, "I came here from heaven for my mother. She needed me. I am teaching her. She really needs me." Dear God, I blushed. I was embarrassed, pleased, proud, and honored.

Following are stories about Laurie's accomplishments, attractions, and challenges. For years, Laurie has won a majority of the games we play with friends or on our private Saturday game afternoons. I seldom give her an advantage! Recently her guard was down, and I heard her whispering a prayer over and over, "Holy Love of God, help me."

I laughed and thought, "That's the secret of her winning. That's how she does it!" She has been in prayer, chanting and winning for years!

At one month of age, Laurie made a droning sound when she lulled herself to sleep. Even then, I labeled it chanting. She still makes the exact sound when she is tired and falling asleep. A few friends have found it annoying. One friend demanded that I move Laurie out of her hearing distance as we visited in her home. I adore the sound and find it comforting and beautiful. To me, it has always been a holy chanting sound.

When Laurie was thirty years old, I discovered that this sound is a well-known nigun. A nigun is a wordless song sung by Hasidic Jews as a means of elevating the soul to God. Because they lacked words, the nigunim were felt to move the singer beyond the sensual and rational, toward the mystic (cited from *Encyclopedia Britannica*). I was preparing to teach the Hebrew dance, "Ev Du," one of the Dances of Universal Peace. Here is an email I sent to Kathryn Ashera Rose, my dance mentor, on December 13, 2006:

> When I was preparing the dance Ev Du, what a trip it was to realize Laurie has been chanting this nigun since she was one month old! Almost every evening, if not every evening, Laurie chants the rhythm with a "ya" sound and a bit of the tune. She was delighted to hear me finally singing it (as I practiced in the living room). She had a self-satisfied look as she peeked around the corner from the kitchen, singing it her way. I realized that she'd been doing this for thirty years and eight months. I gasped, "Oh, that's what you have been doing since you were one month old! Isn't it?"
>
> She nodded, giggled, and smiled. She looked at me as if to say, "Well now! You finally got it!" A little

later, she emphatically showed me how I should teach the dance, with people breaking apart and dancing freely in couples, turning passionately. Next time!

I remember tonight that I was once told by Peter Kempers, a Dutch psychic advisor/healing teacher, to not treat her like a saint. He told me, "Stop being in awe of her, act like a parent, and make sure she knows who is boss and parent this lifetime.

But somewhere, Kathryn, I've taken her (mastery) too much for granted. Certainly I don't take the healing energy in her blessed hands for granted. They always have the power to melt me. But this energy of Murshid Sam that she conveys so often, I really want to honor and value without being inappropriate. What a joy to live with this wise Jewish/Buddhist/Sufi teacher! In Buddhist circles and Sufi circles, she is usually respected. Interesting that her Jewish family rejects her!

As Laurie turned four, the county school system needed to have Laurie's "less-than-perfect material" tested. A psychologist came and administered the Stanford Binet Intelligence Test to Laurie at our kitchen table. He and Laurie sat opposite each other on the benches of our kitchen nook. I sat and observed from the chair at the end of the table as he directed.

The colors of the testing pieces were dull. They certainly couldn't compete with brightly colored Fisher-Price toys that Laurie enjoyed. It was obvious that Laurie was not interested in the psychologist or the test. He was wearing a dull brown suit and a boring tie. Because he asked so many questions, I observed how much she really hated to be questioned. Normally, two questions in a row aggravated her. You can imagine what irritation and fire became dredged up with many questions being directed at her. I interrupted her response to him, "Laurie's getting angry. She hates to be questioned." The psychologist scowled at me. He did not seem to notice and did not seem to care. He had a job to do, and he was going to do it.

When he finished his analysis, he drew his graph of intelligence from Psychology 101 for me. Then, talking down to me, he reported that Laurie tested below dull normal. His findings were that she was very retarded. He had put Laurie's intelligence on the graph at 45. As soon as he finished his sentence, Laurie stood on the bench, put her hands on the table, and determinedly leaned into the middle of the table. She looked him square in the face, squinted her eyes, and blew him a very loud splatter-y raspberry. While he wiped his face, I laughed out loud and said, "Well, I think that's what she thinks of your IQ score."

He looked stunned. He was incapable of believing this "very retarded child" he just tested could express this opinion to him! He was sure that her behavior was rude and accidental. I knew the Mini-Master had "spoken." Laurie and I were both relieved to get him out of our home!

When we first moved to the Netherlands, she was given another IQ test in English. It was administered by a Dutch psychologist and a doctorial student observer in our living room. They requested that I stay in another room. I was puzzled when they finished quickly. They reported with caring in their voices that Laurie became angry when she was asked questions. "Did she experience a trauma today? Is this normal?" I assured the lead psychologist that this behavior was normal. Not wanting to make everyone uncomfortable, I did not tell them that my intuition attributed this personality trait to a past life of interrogation for spying or a bullying parent.

You can imagine how relieved I was to find that they were skilled observers. I continued, "I attempt to hold conversations with her without asking questions." They said because Laurie hated being questioned, that it was, of course, impossible to get a legitimate IQ score. From observing her, they surmised that Laurie was just below the dull normal level of intelligence.

This was definitely not the first or last time in the Netherlands and later in Norway that I felt reassured and comfortable with professionals. The teachers, psychologists, principals, nurses, doctors, social workers, and professionals in general whom we met in Europe were more considerate than their U.S. counterparts. They listened and respected their clients and the family members of special needs children. They encouraged equality and partnership with clients and families. They actually seemed to believe that the mother knew the child better than they did. What a relief to not be belittled or insulted.

From eight to ten, Laurie was obsessed with *Little Red Riding Hood*. She requested the story be read, told, or acted out several times every night! I forced myself to create many versions, to use accents, to discover different angles, and to tell the story from every character's point of view. I even found a musical version to keep from going stir-crazy while repeating this fairy tale every night. We visited Efteling, the largest theme park in the Netherlands, toward the end of her Little Red Riding Hood addiction. In their Fairy Tale Land, there is an exquisite version of grandmother's house. It is approximately one fourth the size, that I imagine an historical grandmother's cottage in the woods would be. Laurie was enchanted and mesmerized. She lovingly peered into the windows, walked around it, and caressed it for over an hour.

I sat patiently waiting on a nearby bench. "Laurie, let's go."

"No, I can't."

Ten minutes later, "Please come, Laurie, people are waiting on us."

Very sweetly, "I'm not finished."

Ten minutes later, "Laurie, are you finished now?"

"No. Where is Little Red Riding Hood?"

"Honey, this isn't like Disneyland." She won't be coming."

"Oh, okay. I love the house!"

"I know, Laurie."

The third time that one of the members of our party came back to check on our progress, I convinced Laurie it was time to join our friends. I think that physical experience with the cottage brought a kind of closure to her obsession with the story. She had seen and touched the place where the little girl with less-than-perfect strength had found success!

Later, I more fully understood her addiction to this particular fairy tale. As we saw more movies together, I recognized that she relishes knowing that the creative innovator, or the little one, or the underdog wins. She absorbs stories in which those who have less-than-perfect material or those with a lesser chance actually win by sheer determination and positive thought. She loves it when those with less-than-perfect material win! Her favorite movies are those in which valiant noble ideas win out. One of her favorites is *The Dead Poet Society*. She also loves *Patch Adams*. Obviously, she also appreciates Robin Williams!

Even though she has not succeeded in getting the paternal family contacts she wants, Laurie almost always gets what she wants. The most irritating example for me was when, for years, she wanted the pink plastic Barbie Doll House. For years, I vehemently said, "*No!*" I finally gave in and had to look at it for two years before she was bored with looking at it also. Happily, it was moved on to another young girl with a pink plastic Barbie obsession.

Laurie also loves the Dick Van Dyke series, "*Diagnosis Murder.*" Healers helping people by doing the impossible with humor, love, and respect is definitely her ideal modus operandi. For several years, she asked me to invite Dick to her birthday party because, as she always said with gusto, "I am his biggest fan!" I never investigated how to do that and continued to feel terribly guilty when I had not followed through with the promise. So, Dick has not made it to one of her birthday parties. Fortunately, at my former position with a nonprofit, I came in contact with the Donor Development Manager at a nonprofit for which Dick entertains in Los Angeles. I shared my dilemma. I asked if she would hand deliver a letter from Laurie to Dick if I sent it to her. She was delighted to help Laurie. "Dick is a wonderful, kind person. He will be here Easter Sunday. Send it, and I will see that he gets it."

Laurie's letter was delivered on Easter Sunday 2006. That morning, Dick Van Dyke left a voice mail while we were at church. After two days and several attempts, he and I successfully set up a telephone appointment. He telephoned Laurie. "Laurie, thank you for being my biggest fan! I want to send you a book. " They talked for four or five minutes. Uncharacteristically, she talked profusely and excitedly. She told him that she loved him and the show!

She was ecstatic. He sent her an autographed copy of *Mr. Finnegan's Giving Chest* by Dan Farr. The character Mr. Finnegan is based on Dick Van Dyke. The inscription of "To Laurie from your friend, Dick Van Dyke, I love you." means so much to her. I noticed today that the book is the first one in her book case. So, as she sits watching TV, she can reach it easily. She continues to admire Dick in this role that demonstrates her healing strategy and intentions.

Because of my career, Laurie has gone to several schools in three countries. Laurie would typically become integrated into a new classroom within a day. She did not need adjustment time. She would walk in, love unconditionally, and start leading. The staff members have assured me at every school she has left that they felt a great loss at her leaving. She becomes half student and half teacher/healer. She brings out potential in students. I am vain enough as her mother to believe she also brings out the potential of the staff. "It won't be the same without Laurie!" is a sentence that I have heard repeatedly when she left a school or training program. She brings a fire, unconditional love, and pizzazz to a group.

I recently remembered another packing/traveling story that I had forgotten. When we first moved to Norway, Laurie became stir crazy during the first dark, Norwegian January. She had not traveled by plane or left the country since the summer. We usually traveled in August and at Christmas time. Laurie often joined me on teaching trips in between. That year we stayed put and entertained in Norway for Christmas.

She kept saying, "Mom, I have to travel"; "I want to fly somewhere"; "Let's go to Holland." I kept giving excuses. She threatened to go to the airport by herself. I hid her passport. Knowing her ability to get places and do things, I thought, "Oh God, I hope nobody would let her get on an airplane without a ticket." I believed that it was not possible; yet I knew of Laurie's determination and ability to get what she wants.

One Saturday morning, Laurie headed out of the door with a packed bag. She said, "Good-bye. I'm going on vacation." She was in the elevator just outside our door before her news sank in. I was not dressed! I panicked. I threw on my boots and wrapped my longest coat over my flannel nightie and caught up to her on the street. Thank God, she was slow in the snow.

She was headed toward a main thoroughfare where people caught buses to the airport! I begged, "Please come back with me. I'll take you on vacation soon." We had no travel budget. I had no teaching tours lined up and wondered what I could possibly do to satisfy her travel yearning. I asked friends for advice.

A friend mentioned that Oslo hotels were hurting and were offering great deals on weekends. I immediately thought of the "pink hotel." Laurie loves hotels. Plus Laurie loves pink houses. So a pink hotel was irresistible to her. When she first saw the Ambassador Hotel, pink with wrought iron balconies in Oslo, she extolled its beauty! It was quite close to our apartment but off the tram/bus route we normally travelled. So she seldom saw the hotel unless we went downtown by taxi. Every time she saw the "pink hotel" she became excited and looked longingly. I strolled over the few blocks to the hotel and told the manager about my dilemma. She gently laughed. "How would you like a suite this weekend?" She gave me a phenomenal price. I accepted! I took the brochure and was delighted to discover that the old luxury hotel had a small pool and a sauna. This would be a great weekend for both of us.

I told Laurie, "We are going on a mini vacation." Secretly I plotted the trip to the hotel. I wanted it to be long enough for her to get bored and ask, "Are we almost there, yet?" I did not want to waste our budget traveling by taxi for that to happen! We would travel by tram.

On Saturday morning, I packed a lunch, juice boxes, and my bag. She packed her bag, a game, two jigsaw puzzles, and a party dress for dinner. We boarded the tram early. I purposely chose to travel in the opposite direction. We even needed to switch trams to get to the pink hotel. About two blocks from the hotel, she whined, "Are we there yet?"

"Almost!"

We ate lunch in and spent the afternoon doing puzzles and playing the game. I enjoyed a spectacular view of the fjord. We indulged in a late and elegant dinner on the town. We celebrated by having a sketch of Laurie done by a street artist. In the 26 hours, we swam three times and took two saunas, and I took two long bubble baths. We relished in a bountiful, fishy-cheesy, Nordic breakfast. It was a satisfying "travel experience" for both of us and just a ten-minute walk from our home. Years later, we poignantly chose to spend our last night in residence in Oslo at the Ambassador Hotel, our "pink hotel."

I realized that we both were suffering from SAD—Seasonal Affective Disorder—caused by the long Nordic nights. Phyllis, the mother of Laurie's friend Alexander, conveniently opened a Light Therapy center. We both were tested for the color that would benefit us. We were both in need of red. Red fires up metabolism and establishes a more grounded energy. I was graciously entrusted with a key to use the center after hours for free. I was grateful for Phyllis's generosity. We went for treatments twice a week. Laurie was cranky, feisty, and belligerent and almost had to be dragged to the bus or tram stop. After a few treatments of red, we both were belligerent, cranky, and feisty and argued constantly. I pleaded with Phyllis for advice. She suggested that we switch to the color green, which creates balance and harmony. Laurie was resistant to go to the Light Therapy center every single time and never agreed to walk there, a one-mile distance. After we switched to looking at the pure green color, Laurie never headed back to the tram/bus stop to go home. Instead she sang, pranced, and danced on ice-packed sidewalks all the way home.

Color therapy definitely helped each of us with our less-than-perfect material. Green worked for us. After two years, I bought two party light bulbs, one pure green and the other blue. We ate breakfast in a ghastly unflattering green glow from October to March. We showered and bathed in a restful blue glow all year.

At age seventeen, Laurie gave me a lesson I did not want. One day, for no reason, she started calling me Ruthann. Initially, I was impressed with this adult quality to our relationship. I became quite upset as it went on for two months or so. I feared that I would never hear the word "mother" again in this lifetime. I was not prepared for that possibility. In fact, it went on for five years. I yearned to hear her call me "mother" again. Moving back to the United States after living abroad for fourteen years unsettled both of us. It put both of us in a state of culture shock (and regression) for several years. Since that time, she occasionally calls me Ruthann, but most of the time I hear "Mom." I sign notes to her sometimes as Ruthann and sometimes as Mom. My heart is always touched with how wisely Laurie addresses greeting card envelopes to me by separating my personhood from the role: "To Ruthann as Mother."

Laurie continues to read my mind, as she has done since she was an infant. I cannot tell you how many times we've been riding silently in the car and she has said, "Stop thinking about …" She is delighted that I have retired from a stressful position at the nonprofit that I could not/did not leave at the office each day. She continues to keep me on track in her simple, perceptive way. And I am grateful that the one with less-than-perfect material acts as a mystery school teacher to me, challenging me and enveloping me in love every day of my life.

14 Power Inside Me

"... power comes from two things, love and peace."

~ Murshid Samuel Lewis

When Laurie was eighteen, Nico van der Vat, one of our dearest friends, passed away from a heart attack. After our discussion of Nico's death, I realized that Laurie had gone through the process of mourning in less than ten minutes. Emotionally and spiritually, I had felt that her grieving was complete. I was astonished. The conversation happened so quickly and I was so involved in my own grieving that I had missed her process. I promised myself that I would observe carefully and learn from her the next time we had a discussion about a death of a friend.

On a teaching trip to Holland in 1994, word came from the United States that Laurie's beloved "Uncle Paul" Solomon had passed away. Feeling concerned for Laurie, I asked the au pair in Norway to let me break the news when I returned. The au pair had not met Paul nor had she experienced Laurie's deep soul to soul relationship to him.

When I returned home, I shared the news with Laurie. My grieving was expressed earlier, and I was prepared for observation. I took mental notes of her grieving process so that I could write it down afterward. I present it here:

Seated closely facing her, I said, "Laurie, I need to tell you something important."

Laurie asked, "What is it?"

I answered, "Uncle Paul is dead. He died in his sleep several days ago."

She took a big breath. Her eyes widened in an expression of shock and disbelief. She needed to check reality by asking, "Uncle Paul is dead? He's really dead?'

I answered, "Yes, Laurie, he died in his sleep."

As if to confirm the news again, she stated, "Uncle Paul is dead."

Tears profusely began to run down her cheeks; she sobbed a few times.

Then Laurie said, "I'll miss him. I loved him." I concurred that I knew that. She paused a bit more than a minute and repeated, "Uncle Paul is dead." Again, she confirmed reality.

She sobbed deeply for about one minute. I held her. She repeated herself a few more times. She became silent with her head bowed for about a minute and said, "God bless him." I knew she had been praying internally for his soul.

Then she looked up smiling and said softly and brightly, "That's okay. Uncle Paul is okay! Uncle Paul is with God!"

Then Laurie laughed saying, "He'll get a new body and he's okay. He's happy."

That was it. She was finished. Again, I was amazed at her grieving speed. I asked, "Are you really okay, Laurie? You wanted to go to see Uncle Paul. I'm sorry you didn't get to see him before he died."

Laurie said, "It's okaaay! He is with God. I'm okaaay!" She said this in a typically dismissive teen voice that we both knew meant, *Enough, leave me alone.*

Two days later and again a week later, I rechecked to see if Laurie was sad about Paul's death. Each time, she smilingly assured me that she was not. "He is okaaay!" she would say, gently dismissing my repeated nosiness. It seemed to me that she was using a Buddhist ideal of not self-cherishing her loss. She was cherishing Paul's all-rightness with God and his prospects of getting a new body.

Laurie completed her mourning in that brief interlude. Only once, eight weeks later, did she say with a bit of regret in her voice, "I miss Uncle Paul."

Probably twice a year, she calmly states, "I miss Uncle Paul."

(I have included my analysis of Laurie's process compared with Elizabeth Kubler-Ross's five steps of grieving in the Appendix.)

We currently live in Northern Virginia. Laurie was three miles from the Pentagon when it was hit by American Airlines Flight 77. Shortly after 9/11 she began to display signs of depression—namely, weight gain and withdrawal from interactions with friends and groups. The previously charming, gregarious young adult suddenly shied away from parties and church. She refused to join her day program field trips, dance classes, and social/church activities she previously relished.

She was working part time in Alexandria on Route 1 at Target in the Potomac Yard Shopping Center as a component of a day program. I was suspicious that she had heard the explosive impact of the plane when she arrived at work by public bus. I knew that she had seen the masses of smoke and had witnessed the mayhem and myriad of people running down the street away from the disaster in the minutes after the crash.

The day program administrators quickly sent a van, picking her up before roads and bridges were blocked. I was thankful that they rushed her back to their venue where I could pick her up. I had already gassed the car, picked up cash from the ATM, and purchased water and basic food supplies. As we headed home, people on main streets were driving their cars on curbs and lawns to get to their families quickly. I moved to side streets. Sirens were blaring from all directions. Laurie was wincing. Even as an infant, she displayed extreme physical discomfort when she heard sirens.

Our apartment was on the path to a hospital from the Pentagon. I knew that she would be further traumatized by the sounds and traffic if we stayed at home. "Laurie, go upstairs and pack quickly. Get your pajamas, some underwear and your sweat suit. We are going to the mountains. It will be cold. I'll get our toiletries." Her packing skills from her toddler years still come in handy. We both packed in less than ten minutes.

I drove out of town by back streets to avoid the continuous sounds of fire truck and ambulance sirens and the impatient horns of people anxious to get to safety. Fire trucks were zipping in from other communities. I am convinced that Laurie felt the pain of the community around her and felt the country's concern. She was obviously in shock. She did not want to talk about "it." I was relieved to be functioning so clearly in my first, and hopefully last, disaster. She wanted the radio turned only to music as we drove. I quickly gave up trying to talk with her about the disaster. I knew she understood that people had died.

I headed for a charming hotel in the mountains that advertised a mid-week special. I had been dreaming of taking advantage of this offer for years. Even though it was not ideal, September 11 was the day my wish came true. In the hotel, Laurie wanted to be alone. She watched the Cartoon Network in our room. I watched the newscasts in the lobby. We came together for meals, games, and comforting each other with hugs. We bought her first Harry Potter book the next morning at the neighboring Wal-Mart. We began reading it in rocking chairs snuggled up together on the large verandah in the brilliant autumn sun. We returned to Arlington late the next evening when the danger seemed to be over.

In typical Laurie fashion, she only opened up a year later as we drove past the Pentagon. Spontaneously, Laurie described with her left arm and hand how the plane swooped down. She imitated the angle of the plane that she would have seen as she climbed out of the bus. Finally, I had verification; she did see the plane make its too-fast descent over the tall buildings in the neighborhood of Rosslyn in Arlington. She quickly said that she saw the plane in the wrong place and heard the crash. End of conversation.

It took nearly two years to work the red tape in the system to get her counseling for depression. Maybe twice, for one minute each, she has talked about "it" since that time. After another three years, her counselor convinced me that Laurie should take a low dose of antidepressants. This might also be called for because she knows and laments that she will not have a "normal life" of marriage, college, and raising children even though she claims normality. We call these pills "the happy pills."

A year ago we met two lovely women in a grocery store. A mother and her Down syndrome–diagnosed daughter who was Laurie's age were strolling around the produce department. We kept meeting them in the different short aisles. After a sweet conversation, we decided that Laurie and I would visit them. We mothers hoped that a friendship would develop. When we arrived, the daughter was reclusive and angry. In order to keep our appointment, her family left a swimming pool earlier than she wished. She pouted and refused to sit in the same room with us. The mother offered us a cool drink. We had a brief and pleasant conversation. The young woman barely said goodbye as we were leaving. As we settled into our car, Laurie looked at me and said, "*SHE NEEDS* happy pills, just like me!" I agreed and we laughed.

It is quite typical of Laurie to pick a big spat with me every two months or so. When she was young, I always tried to do my peace-lover's magic and dispel the energy. She would keep picking and squabbling until we argued. I recognize this pattern as her way of releasing pent up emotions. If I fight her Aries fire with my pumped up weaker fire, we create this big blow up of dragon steam. And when it seems like the argument cannot escalate any higher, Laurie will let out a one-liner of pain that she has had tucked away in her subconscious. At least once a year, the one-liner is, "I am normal!" She then continues to open up, "People don't think I am normal. People look at me funny." And then she sobs, releasing her sorrow. We hug and cry together. The feelings are released for another few months.

She loves to be independent and is especially happy if I have somewhere to go on Saturday evenings. Saturday is "Her Day." Each and every Saturday, she smiles and declares, "This Is My Best Day Ever." She wakes me up by tickling my feet at 7:00 a.m. so that I can get ready to teach piano lessons. She does not dress and will not leave our condominium. We watch two or three cooking shows, cuddle happily in the afternoon, and then play cards for a half hour or so. If I stay home in the evening, she insists that I not cook in the kitchen from 6:00 p.m. to 6:30 p.m. That is *her* time to prepare spaghetti.

Laurie relishes being creative and working as a weaver or textile artist. Thankfully, we arrived back in the states just in the nick of time for me to work the system here to have Laurie graduate from a local school. Graduating from a local high school allowed her to go almost immediately into a day program of weaving. If we had come back a few months later, she would have been too old for public schooling and would not have benefited from the passel of social workers and agencies to find her additional study and or work. She would have been isolated, watching TV for two or more years while waiting for an appropriate training or work program. She was caringly administered to by a team of teachers, case workers, advisors, and more who attempted to find work for her so that she could earn a livelihood and feel fulfilled.

Laurie sabotaged two of the jobs that her advisors arranged for her. She did not know how to say to all of us who were working so hard to find suitable employment for her, "Hey, don't you get it? I am an artist, and I need to create." She lost a job at The Kennedy Center ushering at the Millennium Stage by applying makeup in public places. I must admit, that was my dream job for her.

She also lost a Safeway grocery store position helping people put groceries in their cars. She knew exactly what would get her fired and set about doing those inappropriate actions. She would hide a soda on a shelf and then would quaff a drink while on duty. Two years later, she did ask maturely to be allowed to quit her job at Target. She was bored. She was only allowed to put candy on display. She found the smell of candy too much to take and yearned to feel more productive.

Within months, a spot opened up in a weaving cottage industry, and she has been contented since that time. Her income is minimal and her heart is happy. Her soul is contented and she is fulfilled. Laurie shared about the value of her weaving career when she was asked to demonstrate at a Textile Museum docents' training. After her demonstration, she asked permission to speak to the docents. Sally Lloyd, then-manager of the cottage industry, allowed this, not knowing what to expect. She trusted Laurie. Sally reported that Laurie actually had all of the docents in tears when she talked about the importance of creative expression, and specifically weaving for fulfillment in her life.

At a reception at Laurie's weaving studio, I met one of the executives of Arlington Services. She stated, "I've heard your name. How do I know of you?"

After I looked at her name badge, I laughed and reminded her of my charm. "Five years ago, I left you messages every day for several weeks. By the end I was screaming into your answer phone, begging you to help me get services for Laurie."

Laurie continues to do much with less-than-perfect material. She travels independently to and from her work as a weaver. Her weaving skills make quantum leaps each year. She adores the encouraging staff and bonds with her colleague weavers. For half a year, I could not imagine why she was leaving for work at 7:30 when her job began at 9:00. Her commute is twenty minutes. I kept trying to convince her to sleep in. "Come on, Laurie. You can leave later and arrive at 8:45."

Finally in exasperation, she explained. "I have to get there! They need me. I make coffee and tea for everyone. I have to leave now!" I finally got it: she was volunteering her time to serve her colleagues each morning. Even though she stays up too late, she volunteers to go in to the studio/store early to make tea and coffee ready for the arrival of others. When I started to volunteer at the studio, at long last I could observe her process. She serves her colleagues individually as they sit around two tables. This must fulfill that love of serving and restaurants that was so apparent when she was a little girl.

Laurie has disproved two myths regarding Down syndrome people. The first is that they stop learning at age twenty-one. The second is that they almost never learn to handle money and numbers. Laurie continues to learn new vocabulary, new skills, and new concepts. She has taught herself to handle money better than I ever dreamed possible. Six months ago, she could not discern which milk or grocery products were less expensive. Now, we are both proud that she can make clever choices to save money. She taught herself this important life skill by working with a calculator every evening. She has notebooks filled with numbers. Throughout one entire notebook she adds a specific number, for instance $40, to the previous number. Currently she is at $3,500,000.00.

Laurie is encouraged to write up sales slips at the weaving studio. This privilege is allowed as part of her long-term goal to own a textile and weaving shop. I am sure these privileges of writing sales slips spurred the urgency to independently study and understand numbers.

Laurie is masterful with color and design. She continues to amaze people with her combinations and choices. She has notebooks filled with colorful weaving combinations. She was first trained as a seamstress of patchwork. Years ago, we would sew one or two days a month for a little business that she ran for Christmas bazaars. Now, we usually sew patchwork gifts one day a year as a team. She designs the pattern and chooses the fabric. I do the cutting and ironing. She does the sewing. I do the finishing. She is the master. I am the assistant.

She is addicted —really addicted—to the internet and watching TV. She fills her evenings with researching TV, movie and musical stars, recipes, countries and she also watches several Anime episodes of different characters. Because of this activity, her reading skills and vocabulary are increasing. She is currently obese with thyroid dysfunction. I am attempting to find the best endocrinologist in the area. I affirm that the perfect doctor is appearing! She is involved with Weight Watchers and sabotages the program too often.

Counting on Laurie's wisdom, clarity, and honesty has been a relief from the real world—especially in DC, which is a notoriously closed city. Certainly, Laurie is not without faults; as she has become older and learned the ways of the world, she has told fibs. Usually, it is in self-defense and toward me when she has overeaten. Yet she is the most authentic person I have ever been with. I cherish her authenticity.

She comes close to being obsessed with Yu-Gi-Oh stories. She has the entire book, magazine, video, and DVD collection, except one DVD. She loves the *Master of the Duel*. She orders the magazines, DVDs, and books before they come out. Before the 2009 recession closed her favorite bookstore, she visited there at lunch on Monday through Friday. The store was small and had no chairs; Laurie would sit on the floor and read with the approval of the manager and clerks, who told me they appreciated her business and respect of books.

Once every two years, I take Laurie to New York City for two days. She is too sensitive to be in the city any longer than that. She enjoys Kinokuniya, a Japanese bookstore on par with Barnes and Noble. On the last trip, Laurie spent five hours in the store browsing much of the merchandise on three floors, reading Anime and Manga comics and making several purchases. A friend asked me what she did for so long and what the interest is. I realized as we chatted that Murshid Sam studied in Japan and enjoyed the culture. Possibly it is a throwback for her/him to be in that restful, elegant atmosphere of the store. Laurie seems enchanted. She often points out beautiful book covers of Japanese art and gardens. I also recall Ji Kwang Dae Poep Sa Nim, a Korean Zen Buddhist teacher, who told me in Oslo nearly 20 years ago that Laurie had a recent lifetime as a "naughty" Japanese nun. I never could relate to that story. Maybe there is something to it. Japanese culture is dear to Laurie, although she never talks of visiting Japan.

I went to Europe for eight days over Thanksgiving. Laurie chose to stay home. Because all of our friends were out of town, Laurie happily had to fend for herself. She cooked, managed the house (not the bills and paperwork), watered the plants, locked the doors, and—as usual—got herself back and forth from work with no supervision. One person stopped in to check the garbage disposal and the state of the kitchen counters and to see if she needed a trip to the grocery store on the fifth day. I am impressed. Thankfully, we live in a secure building with a 24-hour desk service in case of emergency. Yes, she is proving that you can do a lot with less-than-perfect material!

Laurie understands that she was lucky to live abroad and privileged to travel as much as she has. She adores flying. This was obvious from the moment she entered a plane at age two with eager excitement and her nose pressed to the window. Her delight at entering an airport and a plane has never wavered. She looks longingly upward when she dreams and talks of going to Hong Kong and Egypt. At least once a month she states, "I want to travel around the world!" I hope she creates many opportunities to get to her desired destinations.

For years, Laurie wanted to live alone in an apartment. Now, she contentedly lives with me. We moved thirty-four times in her first twenty-one years as I was reassigned in the spiritual community and in teaching. She never complained and always seemed cheerful on our spiritual path, as we moved from room to room or apartment to apartment or city to city or country to country. We had been settled in one apartment for eight and a half years when I bought a condominium. As we were packing, she finally complained emphatically. "Don't ever move me again! You have moved me too many times! You always moved me!"

I agreed, apologized, and thanked her for her flexibility throughout the years. She truly aided my career. The tables are turned. I now aid her career. Her position in the weaving studio is dependent on our living in our community which is one of the most expensive suburbs in the United States.

Power Inside Me

As I age and am questioned by people about how Laurie will be cared for after my passing (which I hope is many long years down the road), I continue to affirm that Corrie Van Loon is accurate—"Do not worry about Laurie. She is a master. Laurie will take care of herself."

Laurie's working situation is nearly perfect. I cannot fault it. The staff is warm, welcoming, clear, bright, educated, flexible, fun and grounded. However, my recent days have been filled with some trepidation as I observe her appointments with people hired by the community to help her socialize being less-than-perfect by my standards. Her second helper was extraordinary, kind and exciting, and excited; each subsequent helper has been less involved, less communicative, and seemingly indifferent. I have also done some ranting and raving about this situation, and—by the way—there have been five workers in a year's time. Our condo receptionist thought that Laurie's caretakers were actually only irresponsible, undependable drivers of vans rather than buddies picking her up for a fun event. My prayer and hope is that Laurie will have perfect care now and after my passing. After these recent experiences, my heart wrenches for all those caretakers of special needs children and elderly parents who face this challenge and want the very best for their loved ones.

Laurie precipitates a time when she can have her "greatest dream": Living in (preferably owning) a huge home with helpful people on a beautiful farm with sheep, horses, cows, goats, dogs, and cats. She wants to live with other people who create artistic crafts, cook, and garden together. The farm would include "her" store where she (and other artistic residents) could sell yarn, woven creations, and other textile arts and crafts. I have explored a number of places of residential living that include most of her wishes. They are outside of her current budget. Camphill Village Kimberton Hills, a biodynamic farm in Pennsylvania, is our favorite choice. We pray that the total dream will come true in the near future. Obviously, the proceeds of this book are going into a trust fund for Laurie's future.

Every January, we each create a Treasure Map, a collage of pictures and affirmations to manifest our wishes for the year. This past February, I found the word "power" in large blue letters in a magazine and cut it out. I knew that the Power card is Laurie's favorite card from the angel deck that we share. I happily showed Laurie the blue formatted word I found. She scrunched her nose up when I asked if she wanted it. "Nooooo! I don't need it! I have power inside me!" I grinned as she walked away singing "The Power of Love" by Celine Dion.

Laurie's teaching continues unexpectedly. One autumn Sunday, I woke Laurie up at 11:00 a.m. "Laurie, please come with me on a day trip today. It's beautiful outside, a gorgeous autumn day. Let's take a short trip and get pumpkins and cider. I want a family day." Being melodramatic I added, "And you and I are all the family we have."

She asked to be alone to ask God if she should go. I was relieved and amused that His answer was "Yes."

On Route 66 driving out of the city, Laurie announced with a mischievous smile, "Oh, look. There goes your uncle." I startled. Then I smiled realizing my resident mystery school master-teacher was making a very significant point. Then she said, "Oh, there are our grandchildren." Next, "There's your father!" "Oh, look. There are our nephews." Soon, "My grandfather just waved back."

I laughed feeling upbraided, enlightened and heart warmed. "You are right, Laurie. Thank you. We do have a large family to love. The whole world is our family."

Nodding and grinning a little smugly, "That's right!"

Normally, people in other cars whom she manages to get to wave to her are just her "friends." That day they were our relatives. Off and on during the trip she waved to more of our universal relatives passing in neighboring cars, lest I forget!

Laurie's stories continue to come to me and they are too numerous to add to this book. This final observation by Laurie's case worker which noted Laurie's work place characterics and accomplishments fills me with pride. From this summary, I am aware of how mindfully and respectfully Laurie leads her life.

> *"Laurie is orderly and works efficiently. She takes great care of her work. She is professional and calls if she is to be late or is taking a day off. She cleans up after herself. She thinks about others. She anticipates what everyone wants and needs. She cares. If the coffee is too hot, she will get an ice cube to cool it for a colleague. She waits for everyone to gather to share snacks. She is becoming more adventurous with her designs. She searches in books for designs and has learned to use two shuttles in weaving. She is independent in setting up her loom. She has a broad outlook on life and is a well-rounded person. All of this makes people want to be with her."*

Laurie's experiences continue to warm my heart and inspire me. I admire Laurie's ability to be present. I admire her perseverance. When she has challenging weaving projects, Laurie remains positive. She often says, "I have to keep on keeping on. It's important to finish. I'll keep on keeping on". I trust that Laurie will keep on keeping on bringing peace, joy, truth, harmony, beauty and loving compassion into the lives of everyone she touches.

Epilogue

The book is written.

Laurie and I are home alone between Christmas and New Year's Day.

Serenely, Laurie offers sweet phrases of love and peace:

In the kitchen

Beside my bed

Kneeling at my chair

In the car

At the store

On the street

She touches me with her warm words and hot healing hands.

I melt and am blessed.

At every blip in life, she is offering words of guidance.

Am I more mindful of her messages now?

Has Laurie really been teaching me so often—everyday?

Is this a holiday phenomenon?

I feel peaceful, yet she says,

"Be peaceful."

"Be gentle."

"We have holiday spirit."

"We have good spirit."

My Name Is Laurie

I relax more deeply.

At the minutest tension she feels in me,
    she cautions firmly yet sweetly,

"Noooow! Get some Christmas spirit!"

"Breathe deeply."

A driver cuts us off. I am silent, yet stiffen.

"Be nice" she coos.

A litany of Zen wisdom streams from her soul.

She soothes every strain I feel.

We call old friends to wish them holiday greetings.

They have visitors—

Three highly intelligent but estranged friends, who were extended family to us,
    Like cousins to her for 20 years.
    Refuse to greet her on the telephone.

She is rebuffed.

We hang up. My heart shatters for Laurie.

Moments later, she passionately declares,

"If they won't talk to me, by God, I'll love them anyway!"

I startle. This is maybe the tenth time I have ever heard her swear.

I say, "That's good spirit from you. We'll love them anyhow."

"Yes, I will!

I agree, "Yes, we will!"

A package doesn't arrive on time. She feels my irritation.

"Be nice," she coos.

Epilogue

"Be sweet."

In the kitchen

Beside my bed

Kneeling at my chair

In the car

At the store

On the street

She touches me with her warm words and hot healing hands.

I melt and am blessed.

At every blip in life, her messages continue throughout the week:

"We have New Year's Spirit."

"Holy Spirit is God's spirit."

On New Year's Day, she announces,

"Let's have *Spirit* all year. We can, you know."

I leave on an errand.

Melodiously Laurie calls after me,

"Have fun. Give love."

Closing the door, I reel enveloped in holiness.

Suddenly, I know —

This *is* the fulfillment of her name.

Laurie Shanti means victory through peace.

"Have fun. Give love."

Appendix: Tools for Empowered Development

As mentioned several times in the book, I was lucky enough to be introduced to numerous tools and methods that strengthened Laurie's development and enhanced mine as her primary caretaker. Most of the techniques fall into the arena of health maintenance, positive thinking, and spiritual advancement. My writing classmates suggested that I write a technical book or self-help book on the topic of raising a special child. I declined the suggestion, because I do not possess that knowledge.

If you are looking for a rich source of references, I suggest that you read *Road Map to Holland* by Jennifer Graf Groneberg. It is a heartwarming memoir. It includes wonderful sources of information for parents raising Down syndrome and other cognitively delayed children. Her bibliography is extensive and current.

Following are the tools and techniques that effectively worked to empower Laurie's development:

Numerology as mentioned in Chapter 1, "My Cosmic C-Movie"

I was quite sure that Laurie's birth number as defined by numerology would match the personality she was revealing to me in the womb. The destiny number is the total of the birthday added and then reduced to the smallest number. Her destiny number is #1. She is an innovator and a leader wherever she has the opportunity. My destiny number is #2 (really #11—which is another story). I am a follower and a counselor by nature. Because the two of us have discordant daily numbers, I used numerology to help the two of us coordinate our daily activities with a chart. That chart has been taped to the inside of our kitchen cabinet for fifteen years. I am sure this is difficult to grasp unless you are already trained in numerology; however, let me share how this is possible. On a "2 day" for me, when I yearn for harmony, I find some way for us to cooperate, because it is a "1 day" for her when she wants to lead me. I cooperate with her suggestions. She gets to decide what we cook for dinner, for instance. On a "2 day" for her and a "3 day" for me, I suggest a harmonious-creative project to do together.

Numerology has been a useful tool in my life. The same friend who visited Barbara Lesnovitch with me introduced me to a customer who frequented her Manhattan Upper West Side bookstore. He was a numerologist. Phyllis gave him my birth date and name along with the names and birth dates of several other friends. After looking at the numbers, I was the only one of Phyllis's friends he wanted to meet.

When we met and chatted, which was more like a grilling from him; it was obvious that he was sorely disappointed in me! He expected me to be a budding priestess, healer, and spiritual teacher. At age thirty-two, I certainly was not creating the quality of life he expected me to be living. Plus, from his conversation with me, I only caught a glimmer of how he believed I should be living. Personally, I imagined I could and would be a great family therapist. However, his stern responses to me and guidance helped me consider that I might have forgotten something. He told me clearly that I was not fulfilling my life's destiny.

In spite of the numerologist's negative reaction, I became fascinated with numerology and have used it since that time. I find it a productive coaching technique to recognize a client's destiny number, personality challenges, talents fulfilled and talents in need of acceptance and development, abilities that might be just under the surface, compatibility with family and partners, and more. A psychologist friend who had explored many therapies for decades told me that the session in which I read the numerology chart of her 32-year-old son was the most productive and beneficial counseling session that she had ever had. She finally understood their troubled relationship. She said, "If only I had this information when he was four or five years old, our relationship would have been different. I would have known how to empower him."

Now, after years of observations when counseling people with numerology, I realize that a seemingly uneventful yet life-altering message or experience often happens one week before or after the 33 and 1/3 birth date. Barbara's stern message came to me when I was 33 and 1/3. The event seems to be an offer from the Universe to get serious about life and serves as a call to the life's destiny and soul commitment. Some people take the Universal offer and, obviously, many people are not aware, letting it pass from the course of their life.

Here is just one example of another universal offer to an individual: A colleague at the nonprofit turned 33 and 1/3. Since she was solidly Christian, I explained that God often sent an offer to someone at that age. I asked her what happened a week before or after that date. She first said, "Nothing." She came back an hour later saying, "Ruthann, you were right! At church they suggested I become a deacon." When I asked if she had accepted, she said, "Yes." She accepted her initiation into her line of spiritual service.

I hope each reader near that age will look ahead to plan for availability or that older readers can review the spiritual offer they received at that age. It might not be too late to accept the offer if it was refused. Spiritual offers and lessons happen at any age. Laurie's presence in my life pushed me into responding more fully to my universal offer of service.

Manifestation as mentioned in Chapter 3, "To Teach Me a Lot!"

Another Fellowship teaching became ingrained in me within weeks of Laurie's birth. That teaching is that the Universe loves a vacuum. When you open a vacuum-packed can of coffee or nuts, you hear the air rush in. The Universe fills that empty space! The Universe appears to wish to fill empty spaces. I am sure you have noticed that it is nearly impossible to leave a drawer or shelf empty. I was told that if you clean out your child's closet (or your own closet for that matter) as soon as he or she has outgrown pieces of clothing and give those items away immediately to someone in need, in the next day or so beautiful clothing the perfect size will undoubtedly come through your door. It worked for Laurie and me.

This technique of manifestation works for anyone at any age. So whether it is clothing or other possessions you tire of and no longer want or need, I advise you to donate them quickly and wait for the more appropriate refill.

It is possible to manifest relationships, jobs, characteristics, and more. My talk on this topic is available for download from www.peacethroughunderstanding.net. The talk is number 16, "Precipitation."

Appendix: Tools for Empowered Development

Massage as mentioned in Chapter 3, "To Teach Me a Lot!"

Paul Solomon gave me specific guidelines for keeping Laurie's neck and pelvis loose. He warned me that the Down syndrome condition might possibly limit movement in those areas. So every evening after her bath, she received a total oil massage. (I used Aura Glow, which is recommended by the Edgar Cayce readings.) I paid particular attention to massaging her neck gently. While she was on her back, I rocked her pelvis up and down several times, usually singing a happy song. While she was on her stomach, I massaged the sacrum area softly. Those moments of massage relaxed both of us and provided a peaceful bonding. As mentioned earlier, Laurie requested the massages to stop at age eight. Her love of dancing has kept her neck and pelvis flexible.

Broadcasting as mentioned in Chapter 5, "To Teach Laurie a Lot"

The technique of broadcasting, which is practical and yet mystical, can be used by a parent or guardian to influence a child's behavior through their subconscious until the age of seven. A child's subconscious is most receptive the few moments before sleep and that is the perfect time to apply this method. Through broadcasting the parent or guardian can plant positive thinking and behavioral choices in the subconscious. Broadcasting can be used for physical, mental, emotional, and spiritual development.

I knew broadcasting would work for Laurie, because after two nights at three and a half weeks of age, she was sleeping through the night with my suggestions. I began to broadcast nightly to her and continued until she turned seven years of age. Nightly I sent Laurie messages of encouragement and empowerment about her physical and mental development. I also used it when Laurie was three years of age and she had developed a habit of biting out of frustration. She bit playmates when they could not understand her speech impediment. The biting phase was short lived.

I am firmly convinced that this broadcasting technique will also work wonders with autistic children, emotionally troubled children, as well as other children with multiple handicaps.

At the age of seven, a child becomes spiritually responsible for his or her own decisions. The ritual of first Communion is used in the Catholic religion to mark this developmental stage. This is recognized in many religions; in astrology, it is one quarter of a Saturn cycle in the birth chart.

I am told that the Cosmic Law is as follows: If your child kills someone before age seven, you will be held responsible. If your child kills someone after age seven, the child is held responsible. Parents are not allowed to interfere with a child's subconscious after this age.

Each night as Laurie was falling asleep; I would say an affirmation that buoyed her development. It went something like this: "Laurie, you are a child of Light, a child of God, you are loved by God. You are now learning to crawl. You are creeping beautifully and soon you will be crawling and having fun. This will be easy for you." I found this undertaking reassuring and fulfilling. I understood that I was working deeply with Laurie's mind and empowering her to faster development. I was always one step ahead of her progress with the technique of broadcasting. She walked at eighteen months and developed much faster than the other Down syndrome children in her infant stimulation class.

Patterning and superlearning as mentioned in Chapter 5, "To Teach Laurie a Lot"

The parents who bring their children to The Institutes of Achievement of Human Potential are taught superlearning skills. For five days, we adults wrapped ourselves in blankets to survive the purposefully controlled 50-degree temperature lecture hall. Dr. Glen Doman, founder of The Institute and now deceased, insisted that is the best temperature for learning. There were exact ten-minute orange juice and coffee breaks on each hour in a warm vestibule. Several friends working toward Masters in Business Administration have told me that they are encouraged as managers to encourage their staff members to take five minute breaks each hour to relieve tension, increase productivity, and prevent stress.

At The Institute children are watched, tested, and observed separately by experts when the parents are in superlearning classes. I came home with an Institute dictate to have three volunteers for each day to administer the program. The most dramatic point of the program was the patterning. A child or baby would have three adults moving his or her body in a creeping or crawling movement. The child would be on his/her stomach. One person would move the head appropriately from side to side and the other two adults would move the legs in the appropriate manner. Once a child became too large to be patterned, they were instructed to crawl for five minutes several times a day.

Laurie's program was as follows:

1. Laurie was patterned by three adults for creeping until she could creep on her own steam. Then she was patterned for crawling. The crawling patterning continued after she could walk because the cross crawling action is beneficial for right/left brain development, which helps with all physical/mental activities.

2. Laurie was taught to read with three-inch-high flash cards of individual words written in red. Red is supposedly an easier color for young eyes to distinguish than black is. The word cards were flashed quickly in front of her, five different times a session, during three sessions a day. The cards were flashed high, low, on the right, on the left, and in a mixed presentation to keep her amused and alert. She was to be presented with five to eight new words a day. Those words were reinforced five days before the words were retired to a review packet. I created a new packet of words every evening after Laurie fell asleep.

3. To recognize amounts of objects, we used ninety-nine large poster board cards with one dot to ninety-nine dots. Five cards were flashed in front of her five different times in each session.

4. There was to be a NEW lesson every day with five or more twelve-inch square poster board cards on some fascinating colorful topic with pictures on one side and brief text on the other side. Usually these lessons were made from old National Geographic magazines or graphic books that I bought at thrift shops and used bookstores. These cards were to be flashed before her five times each day. All of this information was flashed quickly to the side or high or low before her with clear diction. Nothing was to be boring. The presentation rhythms were to be varied in speed and location around her.

5. She was also to be deeply breathed by two people pulling dowels threaded through a specially made vest to fit her. The "vest" wrapped around her and overlapped with an inch gap for

Appendix: Tools for Empowered Development

inhalation and exhalation. After observing her breathing pattern, experts at The Institute had advised how many seconds to let her breathe out and how many seconds to let her breathe in. We sang little ditties to keep the exact rhythm. We sang as we kept the rhythm going. I cannot tell you many times I have sung "Michael, Row the Boat Ashore" and "Row, Row Your Boat."

6. Another part of The Institute training was the plastic mask mentioned in the text.

Laurie was patterned for two-plus years by volunteers who learned to love her and learned how to present the lessons I developed and constructed every evening. Lessons were pulled after five days and put into an historical file that would then be put into circulation again for reviews. As an infant, Laurie had lessons on many topics: most breeds of dogs and cats, many other animals, wild flowers, whales in the Arctic, gold mining, Fiji Islanders, and more. Information was put in and was never expected to be pulled out. Laurie was occasionally tested by putting two words in front of her and asking her one word. She would look at the correct word and not be expected to speak it.

The Use of Buttons as per kinesiology and mentioned in Chapter 5, "To Teach Laurie a Lot"

The first summer that we lived in Holland, we stopped to stretch our legs at a little village playground on a Sunday tour. There was a small trampoline at ground level with a pit underneath it. Laurie instantly realized that this trampoline was safe for her and jumped onto it. She could not jump more than once before she would fall. She tried over and over. She came off the trampoline crying in desperation. She ran into my arms, "I can't do it, Mommy. I can't do it."

My heart quivered for her. I thought, we have nothing to lose if I do "The Buttons" on Laurie.

The day before, I had received a healing session with Yoke Brouwer, who is a master of Applied Kinesiology techniques and an intuitive healer. Yoke balanced my energies and tested me for supplements. During our session, she taught me three exercises she called "The Buttons." "Ruthann, please learn "The Buttons" carefully. In your work, you'll meet many people who will need them. They are simple to teach and they help people become more balanced and effective."

I immediately experienced and understood that the "The Buttons" balance the energies of both the body and the mind.

Laurie resisted a bit this first time I used "The Buttons" on her. She said they tickled. Then she decided to trust me after I explained the little rubs might help her jump better. This process takes less than three and a half minutes, even with a resistant wiggly eight year old. I applied light pressure to "The Buttons" on her body. Immediately, she ran back to the trampoline. She actually jumped for three minutes continuously before she needed another button fix. It seemed like a miracle! Each time she came back smiling, "I can do it! I can do it." We were both thrilled. I understood the effectiveness of using this technique for Laurie, others, and me.

In the days afterward, Laurie learned to do "The Buttons" for herself. We both used them daily for years. I think they are helpful for almost *everyone* once or twice a day. I describe the feeling I have after doing them as feeling firmer in my skin and more connected to my body. Obviously, I feel more integrated. I just discovered while writing this section of the book that Laurie still remembers these three exercises and uses them at her own discretion.

Years later when I was introduced to *Brain Gym Games*, I thought Yoke had taught me the exact *Brain Gym Buttons*. Upon doing research for the book, I found that they are slightly different. I am describing them in the following paragraph as I remember Yoke teaching them to me 25 years ago. It seems that *Brain Gym* developed out of Applied Kinesiology. I recently met another skilled Kinesiologist who did "The Buttons" exactly as Yoke did.

Following is my order, which may not be the recommended order by a skilled trainer.

First Exercise: Put a fingertip in the navel—through clothing is fine. Being trained in Polarity Therapy when I work the upper part of the body, I put the right index finger in the navel and with the left hand use the index and middle fingers to massage the points on the front of the collarbone on either side of the throat indentation. Alternate the pressure between the two areas of contact. I understand that this button aligns the right and left hemispheres of the brain. Continue for one minute alternating pressure. If you yawn, or cough, or belch or let out air in any other manner, it is a good sign. Know that you are releasing tension and finding balance.

Second Exercise: Keep that same fingertip on the navel and with the other hand hold the upper and lower lips between the index finger and thumb, wiggling and tugging them gently, rest and massage the navel and then the lips in alternating movements. This button, I am told, balances the energies above and below the waist. Again, alternating the pressure for a minute is enough.

Third Exercise: Keep one fingertip in the navel (I put the left middle finger in the navel at this point) and the right index finger on the tip of the coccyx. Doing the "The Buttons" through clothing is fine. Again, you alternate pressure between these two points for a minute. This button balances the energies in the front and back of the body.

In just three minutes by repeating each exercise with alternating soft pulsing pressure on each point for five to ten seconds, your body becomes temporarily aligned.

My greatest success from using "The Buttons" was with a Dutch doctoral student in mathematics who had been struggling with exams and his Ph.D. dissertation for eight years. His frustrated mother gifted him with three coaching sessions with me. She was hoping I would "fix him" with my psycho-spiritual counseling. It was "The Buttons" that he used four or five times a day that successfully helped him finish the dissertation in a year and a half! When he learned to recognize that he was out of alignment, he applied "The Buttons" as he needed. He then entered into a "groove of effective functioning," as he called it.

There are many *Brain Gym* exercises available in several books. Please see the bibliography. My long time friend, Jerry V. Teplitz, JD, Ph.D., has written *Switched-On Living* with Norma Eckroate and I find it invaluable for me personally. His *Brain Gym for Business* co-authored with Gail and Paul Dennison is useful. The Dennison's have written a small book for children just called *Brain Gym*. I suggest that all families with special needs children have this book in their library.

Appendix: Tools for Empowered Development

Grieving, Laurie style, as mentioned in Chapter 14, "Power Inside Me"

After observing Laurie's mourning process, I felt compelled to compare it with Elizabeth Kubler-Ross's five steps of grieving.

Elizabeth Kubler-Ross lists five normal steps most people go through in grieving in her book *On Death and Dying*: 1. Denial, 2. Bargaining (with God doctors, time, etc.), 3. Anger, 4. Depression, 5. Acceptance. She states that these stages are important in the acceptance of a life-threatening disease to oneself or to a loved one.

I believe Buddhists would consider many of Kubler-Ross's steps as "self-cherishing attitudes" that cause pain. Laurie's attitude, which is so effective, is mostly other-cherishing. Laurie profoundly understands that there is the great "bargain" of getting a new body and being with God. She seems to skip over the second stage of bargaining with earthly beings, the announcer of the death, doctors, nurses, friends, and family. I understand that this might be different if my life was in peril.

Laurie does not experience anger while grieving. It's common knowledge that anger is generally an attempt to control others. We feel anger when we are out of control or attempting to regain control. She does not have to try to control reality or the departed with her power or anger. Laurie allows the other soul to choose their leave taking. Because Laurie is not falsely attached to just one person here and one person there, she seems to be able to unconditionally accept an individual's choice of transition.

Because Laurie fully allows her sorrow, she skips the depression stage that is often delayed. Laurie is not ashamed to cry deeply. She releases her sorrow immediately. She does not closet any of her grief, and therefore, it does not swamp her later and has no chance to poison the chemistry of her body.

On top of the acceptance, Laurie quickly accesses her superconsciousness or Inner Teacher/soul by praying. Remember that she prayed for Paul after his surprise death (in his sleep) and checked out his "okay-ness" with her intuition? Her concern was for Paul being with God and Paul getting a new body. She was cherishing Paul and not herself. She decided to be happy about his transition.

I studied communication with Virginia Satir. At that time she talked about five steps of communication. Laurie follows those steps naturally by using the wisdom of her five lower chakras. Here is the pattern she used:

1. She heard the fact of the death and confirmed it.
2. She thought it was difficult to accept and needed to hear it several times.
3. She felt and expressed her sorrow.
4. She believed that Paul was with God and had a new body
5. She decided to be joyful in knowing he was "okaaaay!"

(I have written a self-help book about "The 5 Steps of Communication," soon to be available on www.peace-throughunderstanding.net.)

Edgar Cayce Remedies

Our daily life in Virginia Beach was so steeped in the wisdom of Edgar Cayce Remedies and health building knowledge that I took it for granted. The external use of Castor oil played an enormous role in our lives. Laurie came home from the hospital with an angry rash from the required silver nitrate eye drops. Two days of castor oil used on her cheeks cured the rash. Castor oil soothed burns and prevented scarring. Castor oil relieved ear aches (I discovered this later in Laurie's life). Castor oil eased sore muscles, sprains and took away minor coughs overnight. It is no wonder that the Dutch refer to Castor oil as "wonder oil." Aura Glow took away pregnancy stretch marks and proved to be a wonderful massage oil. Glycothymoline proved invaluable in our medicine cabinet. Cayce's advice on eating an alkaline diet has helped us create vital health. Edgar Cayce's advice on dreams, meditation and spirituality is uplifting and empowering.

Cranial Adjustments

When Laurie was thirteen, we met a dedicated chiropractor in Norway. Dr. Knut Åsjer taught us about cranial adjustments. I think the adjustments were helpful. We all agreed that we would have achieved great benefit if the process had begun earlier. After a year and a half, Laurie and I both dropped the daily routine of pushing on specific points on her head and in her mouth. Knut shared that this technique was recommended for babies with Down syndrome. If you choose to go this route, please tread carefully and be completely assured of the chosen practitioner.

Food Supplements

Immediately after Laurie's birth, Paul Solomon informed me about the work of Dr. Henry Turkel, MD of Detroit. He was the pioneer on nutritional supplements for Down syndrome. While Laurie was nursing, I took many supplements that Dr. Turkle suggested for growth and development. After she stopped nursing, I made peanut butter balls for Laurie with ground-up supplements. No matter how much maple syrup I added, they still tasted bitter and unappealing to me. Laurie did not mind. In fact she liked them. From age five on, Laurie could swallow a handful of supplements at a time. I gladly resigned my job as tablet-grinder and maker of nutritional peanut butter balls. Throughout Laurie's life, I have spent hundreds of dollars a year on supplements for her. I am convinced they work. I notice that when I stop or slow the supplementation, her reading ability decreases and her understanding in general become duller.

When we were in Holland, I managed to get a prescription from our family doctor for pure amino acids manufactured in Germany and sold in glass vials. Laurie was delightfully alert and physically active when she took them. When we moved to Norway, they were not available there. The dear Dutch pharmacist kept Laurie supplied with them for two or three years afterward as I commuted between the two countries. The pharmacist and I lost touch and Laurie lost this wonderful product. The odor from the vial nauseated me and gladdened Laurie. She loved the taste. She did very well in all areas of her life when she took these pure amino acids. Unfortunately, I've not found any supplementation here in the United States that equals that high quality.

Glossary of Names and Terms

All in the Family: An American television situation comedy that ran from 1971 to 1979.

"Amma," Amritanandamayi, Mata: Indian Yogini born September 27, 1953; the "Hugging Saint"; author; founder of schools and hospitals; recognized by the United Nations.

Ananda: The Hindu name translates as bliss; it is considered the highest state of being.

A.R.E.®: Association for Research and Enlightenment, Inc. (A.R.E.®), a nonprofit organization founded in 1931 by Edgar Cayce (1877-1945) to research and explore transpersonal subjects: holistic health, ancient mysteries, personal spirituality, dream interpretation, intuition, philosophy and reincarnation.

Arica School (or Arica Institute): Founded by Oscar Ichazo; presents practical and theoretical knowledge in training programs called scientific mysticism.

Aura Glow: A formula containing pure peanut, olive, lanolin, and vitamin E oils. Edgar Cayce recommended Aura Glow to beautify the body and to enhance flexibility.

"Babaji," Mahavatar Babaji: Born 203 A.D.; a Christ-like Indian saint; reportedly lived for centuries in the Himalayas, guiding spiritual teachers at a distance; taught "Kriya Yoga," to Lahiri Mahasaya who initiated others, including Yogananda's guru, Sri Yukteswar.

Bach Flower Remedies®: Natural, dilute solutions made from spring water, an alcohol preservative, and the parts of specific flowers; used to bring about a state of equilibrium in living organisms.

Bach, Marcus, Ph. D. (1906-1995): Recognized as a leading authority on the world's religions and intercultural relations; author of twenty-seven books.

Baker-roshi, Zentatsu Richard: Born Richard Dudley Baker, March 30, 1936; an American Soto Zen roshi; dharma Heir of Shunryu Suzuki-roshi.

Barodofsky, Murshid Saul Yale (Hakim Sauluddin): A disciple of Murshid Samuel Lewis; director of the Ruhaniat Dervish Healing Order since 1977.

Beautiful Painted Arrow: See Rael, Joseph.

Brain Gym®: Developed by Paul and Gail Dennison in the 1970s to help learning disabled children and adults consists of twenty-six physical activities used to bring about rapid improvements in concentration, reading skills, writing, athletic skills and well-being.

Brouwer, Joke: Dutch Kinesiologist and master teacher of several modalities of healing.

Bunker, Archibald "Archie": A reactionary, bigoted, conservative fictional character played by Carrol O'Connor in the American television situation comedy *All in the Family*.

Byer, David: Internationally recognized dancer based in Norway; dance teacher and choreographer; graduate of the Caribbean School of Dancing.

Carmel In The Valley: From 1979-1981, a large spiritual community in the Shenandoah Valley, sponsored by The Fellowship of The Inner Light; later a smaller retreat center on thirteen acres. The colonial style house was referred to as Hearthfire Lodge.

Carson, John William "Johnny": (1925-2005) Comedian and television host, best known for "The Tonight Show Starring Johnny Carson," who was a Kennedy Center Honoree in 1993.

Carter, Jeffrey: Internationally recognized dancer based in Norway and France; dance teacher, and choreographer; graduate of the Caribbean School of Dancing.

Charlton, Hilda: (1906-1988) Spiritual teacher, author, dancer, and healer who taught meditation classes in New York City for 23 years.

Dagpo Rinpoche: Recognized at age two by the thirteenth Dalai Lama as the reincarnation of Dagpo Lama Jampel Llundrup, also recognized as the reincarnation of Marpa the Translator. Taught Tibetan language and Buddhism at the School of Oriental Studies, a part of the Sorbonne from 1961-1993; author; founder of numerous international Dharma centers.

Dalai Lama, The: Born July 6, 1935, His Holiness the fourteenth Dalai Lama, Tenzin Gyatso, is spiritual leader of Tibet; recognized at age two as the reincarnation of the thirteenth Dalai Lama, Thubten Gyatso.

"Dark night of the soul": A phase in life marked by a sense of loneliness and desolation.

Dennison, Paul and Gail: See Brain Gym®.

Down syndrome: Also called trisomy 21; Down syndrome is the most common chromosome abnormality. It is caused by the presence of an extra chromosome 21, and sometimes by the translocation of chromosome 14 or 15 and chromosome 21 or 22. There are varying degrees of delays in physical development and multiple cognitive defects. The incidence of Down syndrome caused by an extra chromosome 21 is one in six hundred to six hundred fifty live births and is associated with maternal age (over 35 years) and can rise to an incidence of one in eighty for mothers over 40 years. Down syndrome caused by translocation is hereditary, the incidence being one in five if the mother is the carrier and one in twenty if it is the father. The third cause of Down syndrome which is the rarer mosaic variant, in which there is a mixture of trisomy 21 and normal cells. This leaves the individual with fewer physical defects and less severe cognitive development. Source: The Harry Spink Foundation.

Findhorn Foundation: A Scottish charitable trust founded by Eileen and Peter Cady and Dorothy Maclean; a spiritual community, eco-village, and international workshop center.

Glossary of Names and Terms

Fuller, Buckminster "Bucky": (1895-1983) Visionary, architect, author, and inventor.

Hazrat Inayat Kahn: (1882-1927) Hazrat Inayat Khan, born in India; author, teacher of Sufism in America and Europe in the early 20th century. He started "The Sufi Order in the West" (now called the Sufi Order International); father of Pir Vilayat Inayat Kahn.

Hearthfire Lodge: A mansion at Carmel in the Valley that housed The Synthesis Program, meditation room, office, and residence of Paul Solomon.

Institutes for the Achievement of Human Potential, The: A nonprofit educational organization specializing in child brain development, serves both brain-injured children and well children.

Kahn, Pir Shabda: Head (Pir) of the Sufi Ruhaniat International; a disciple of Murshid Samuel Lewis; lecturer, musician, and leader of Dances of Universal Peace.

Kempers, Peter: Deceased spiritual teacher, intuitive healer and psychic; operated a center in the Netherlands from the late 1970s until moving to the Dutch Antilles in the early 1990s.

Khan, Pir Vilayat Inayat: (1916-2004) Head of the Sufi Order International for over fifty years; taught the traditions of the East Indian Chishti Order of Sufism; author of numerous books. *Toward the One* served as a handbook for spiritual seekers in the 1970s.

Kjeldsrud, Anne Brit: Dancer and teacher of modern dance, graduate of the Norwegian Opera Ballet School, a major influence in Norwegian modern dance for several decades.

Kübler-Ross, Elisabeth: (1926-2004) Swiss born psychiatrist, researcher, and writer in the field of thanatology, known for her theory of the five stages in the dying process. Her most admired books are *On Death & Dying* and *The Dougy Letter—A Letter to a Dying Child*.

Lahiri Mahasaja: (1828-1898) Householder Indian guru; teacher of the ancient Indian art of Kriya Yoga, known for breaking down caste barriers; guru to Swami Sri Yukteswar.

Lee, Peggy: (1920-2002) Singer, songwriter, actor.

Lesnovitch, Barbara: Minister and psychic who practiced in New York City in the 1970s.

Lewis, Murshid Samuel L.; Sufi Ahmed Murad Chisti: (1896-1971) Gardener, scholar, author; spiritual leader of the hippies in San Francisco, CA; recognized as a Sufi and Zen master; developed dances that later led to the origination of the Dances of Universal Peace.

Linden, Saphira: Transpersonal psychotherapist, Sufi senior teacher, Cheraga *(Sufi minister) and a cofounder of the Chrysalis Connection, Artistic Director of Omega Theater, Boston.

Marlow, Mary Elizabeth: International transpersonal teacher, author, and intuitive counselor.

Meher Baba (1894-1969), born Merwan Sheriar Irani, was an Indian mystic and spiritual master. He was one of the first Indian gurus who taught in the West.

Mosaic variant of Down syndrome: See Down syndrome.

Mother Meera: Born Kamala Reddy on December, 26, 1960, in India; believed by many to be an embodiment of the Divine Mother; lives in Germany; travels internationally.

Mystery School: A school for the study of human inner nature, the earth, and the wisdom of spiritual traditions. Students strive to develop a pure relationship with divinity through self-discipline and devotion to become at one with his/her inner light.

Ninety-Nine Names of God: Many of the names used by Muslims and found in the Qur'an have Semitic roots. Each name represents a characteristic of God.

O'Kane, Thomas Atum, Ph. D.: International teacher; graduate of the Guild for Spiritual Guidance; integrates the psychology of Carl Jung, the vision of Teilhard de Chardin, and the practice of Christian Mysticism; past Secretary General of the Sufi Order International.

"Papa Nico": Nico van der Vat (deceased), board member of Peace Through Understanding. When Laurie met this private healer and humanitarian, she began to call him "Papa Nico."

Paramahansa Yogananda: (1893-1952) Founder of Self-Realization Fellowship, one of the first Indian gurus to come to the West; author; taught the underlying unity of the world's religions and methods for attaining direct experience of God.

Patterning: Three people move the body of the subject in a creeping or crawling movement on his/her stomach; one person moves the head, two people move the legs.

Peace Through Understanding: An educational organization founded by Ruthann Pippenger and students in the Netherlands in 1985; offering psycho-spiritual tools and techniques to safely open up and create peace, joy, truth, harmony, and beauty in relationships.

Perls, Laura and Frederick: Psychotherapists at the Frankfurt Psychological Institute; fled Nazi Germany during 1933. *Ego, Hunger and Aggression*, published in 1942, introduced their new theory of psychotherapy, Gestalt Therapy.

Pir: a grade in the spiritual hierarchy of Hazrat Inayat Kahn. "The work of a *Pir* is helping individuals toward the unfoldment of their soul."

Poep Sa Nim, Ji Kwang Dae: Founder of the Yun Hwa Denomination of World Social Buddhism teaches internationally; established the Lotus Buddhist Monastery in 1993.

Glossary of Names and Terms

Rael, Joseph, known also as Beautiful Painted Arrow: An international author, artist, visionary, storyteller of the Ute and Picuris Pueblo Indian traditions.

Rose, Kathryn Ashera: Mentor of Dances of Universal Peace; Creator of Family Dance Camps; author/editor of Books and CDs: *I Open My Eyes to You* and *All My Relations.*

Rosner, Jorge: Ran Gestalt groups in Chicago in the late 1960s; incorporated drama, bodywork, and Buddhism into his work; founded international Gestalt institutes.

Rudolf Steiner Helsepedagogisk Skole: See Rudolf Steiner.

St. Denis, Ruth: (1877-1968) American dancer, choreographer, one of the founders of modern dance; collaborated with Murshid Samuel Lewis. They combined simple dance movements with prayers, chants, scriptures, and holy phrases set to music.

Satir, Virginia: (1916-1988) Called the Mother of Family Therapy; founded the Mental Health Research Institute (MHRI) in Menlo Park with Don Jackson and Jules Riskin; first Director of Training at Esalen Institute of Big Sur, California; author, international consultant to schools, hospitals and mental health agencies. Books include *Self Esteem*, *Making Contact, Your Many Faces, Conjoint Family Ttherapy, The New Peoplemaking.*

Sri Chinmoy: (1931-2007) Indian Spiritual teacher, musician and artist.

Singh, Tara: (1919-2006) Spiritual teacher, yogi and author; proponent of *A Course In Miracles.*

Solomon, Paul: (1939-1994) Founder of the Fellowship of the Inner Light; Creator of Inner Light Consciousness course; psychic, visionary; author of numerous books.

Steiner, Rudolf: (1861-1925) Austrian author, architect; founded Anthroposophy, a philosophy growing out of European Transcendentalism with links to Theosophy; with others developed Waldorf education, biodynamic agriculture, and anthroposophical medicine.

Stellium: A multiple astrological conjunction involving three or more planets in one house and/or one sign in an astrological chart.

Sufism: A variety of mystical paths designed to ascertain the nature of mankind and God and to facilitate divine love and wisdom in the world. Sufism arose after the death of Muhammad (A.D. 632) among different groups who found orthodox Islam to be spiritually stifling.

Superlearning: A system to help people learn large amounts of information quickly; outlined in a 1979 book by Sheila Ostrander and Lynn Schroeder with Nancy Ostrander.

Swami Muktanada: (1908-1982) Indian Hindu guru; founder of Siddha Yoga.

Swami Sri Yukteswar: (1855-1936) India householder guru, disciple of Lahiri Mahasaya; guru to Paramahansa Yogananda, author of *The Holy Science*.

Ton, Jan: the Netherlands; lecturer, author on Tarot, astrology, I Ching, and dreams. Senior teacher for Peace Through Understanding retreats; creator of the game, *Tarot Labyrinth*.

Trevelyan, Sir George: (1906-1996) International lecturer; explored the effects of crystals; the power of ley lines, and organic farming; founded the Wrekin Trust to promote spiritual education; awarded the Right Livelihood award (the 'alternative Nobel Prize').

Turkel, Henry, MD: Started treating the metabolic disorders of Down syndrome in 1940 with a mixture of vitamins, minerals, fatty acids, digestive enzymes, lipotropic nutrients, glutamic acid, thyroid hormone, antihistamines, nasal decongestants, and a diuretic.

Van Loon, Corrie: Internationally recognized as a spiritual teacher, psychic and healer.

Vigeland Park, Oslo, Norway: Covers an area of eighty acres. Two hundred twelve sculptures by Gustav Vigeland. The sculptures are divided into five main units: Main Entrance, The Bridge area, The Fountain, The Monolith Plateau, and The Wheel of Life.

BIBLIOGRAPHY

Angel Unaware by Dale Evans Rogers, 1953, Revell.

Awakening: A Sufi Experience, Part 1 by Pir Vilayat Inayat Khan, 1999, Penguin Putnam, Inc.

Brain Gym™ by Paul E. Dennison, Ph.D., and Gail E. Dennison, 1986, Edu-Kinesthetics, Inc.

Brain Gym™ *for Business* by Paul E. Dennison, Ph.D., Gail E. Dennison, and Jerry V. Teplitz, J.D., Ph.D., 1994, Edu-Kinesthetics.

The Edgar Cayce Remedies by William A. McGarey, MD. 1983, Bantam Books

Expecting Adam by Martha Beck, 1999, Berkley Books.

How a Master Works by Ivy Oneita Duce, 1975, Sufism Reoriented, Inc.

Infant Massage by Vimala Schneider McClure, 2000, Bantam Revised.

In the Garden by Murshid Samuel L. Lewis, reprinted 2009, PeaceWorks Publications.

The Miracle Oil by David E. Kukor, 2008, A.R.E. Press

Murshid by Mansur Johnson, 2006, PeaceWorks Publications.

The New Peoplemaking by Virginia Satir, 1988, Science and Behavior Books, Inc.

Road Map to Holland by Jennifer Graf Groneberg, 2008, New American Library.*

Switched-On Living™ by Jerry V. Teplitz, J.D. Ph.D. with Norma Eckroate, 1994, Happiness Unlimited Publications.

Touch for Health by John F Thie, D.C., and Mary Marks, 1973, De Vorss and Company.

World Gender Gap,
    http://www.guardian.co.uk/world/2010/oct/12/world-gender-gap

* For parents of Down syndrome children, I recommend consulting the outstanding Resources section of Jennifer Graf Groneberg's book, *Road Map to Holland*.

uct-compliance

BIBLIOGRAPHY

Angel Unaware by Dale Evans Rogers, 1953, Revell.

Awakening: A Sufi Experience, Part 1 by Pir Vilayat Inayat Khan, 1999, Penguin Putnam, Inc.

Brain Gym™ by Paul E. Dennison, Ph.D., and Gail E. Dennison, 1986, Edu-Kinesthetics, Inc.

Brain Gym™ *for Business* by Paul E. Dennison, Ph.D., Gail E. Dennison, and Jerry V. Teplitz, J.D., Ph.D., 1994, Edu-Kinesthetics.

The Edgar Cayce Remedies by William A. McGarey, MD. 1983, Bantam Books

Expecting Adam by Martha Beck, 1999, Berkley Books.

How a Master Works by Ivy Oneita Duce, 1975, Sufism Reoriented, Inc.

Infant Massage by Vimala Schneider McClure, 2000, Bantam Revised.

In the Garden by Murshid Samuel L. Lewis, reprinted 2009, PeaceWorks Publications.

The Miracle Oil by David E. Kukor, 2008, A.R.E. Press

Murshid by Mansur Johnson, 2006, PeaceWorks Publications.

The New Peoplemaking by Virginia Satir, 1988, Science and Behavior Books, Inc.

Road Map to Holland by Jennifer Graf Groneberg, 2008, New American Library.*

Switched-On Living™ by Jerry V. Teplitz, J.D. Ph.D. with Norma Eckroate, 1994, Happiness Unlimited Publications.

Touch for Health by John F Thie, D.C., and Mary Marks, 1973, De Vorss and Company.

World Gender Gap,
    http://www.guardian.co.uk/world/2010/oct/12/world-gender-gap

* For parents of Down syndrome children, I recommend consulting the outstanding Resources section of Jennifer Graf Groneberg's book, *Road Map to Holland*.

www.ingramcontent.com/pod-product-compliance
Lightning Source LLC
LaVergne TN
LVHW081449070426
835507LV00018B/2056